Brave Women Write

On facing grief, finding hope
and freeing the writer within.

*A powerful manifesto for women who yearn to
write for both personal and planetary change.*

CAROLYN TATE

This edition published by Carolyn Tate 2022

ISBN 978-0-6456094-0-0

Copyright © 2022 Carolyn Tate. All rights reserved.

No part of this publication may be reproduced, distributed, or transmitted in any form or by any means, including photocopying, recording, or other electronic or mechanical methods, without the prior written permission of the publisher, except in the case of brief quotations embodied in critical reviews and certain other non-commercial uses permitted by copyright law. For permission request, contact the publisher, Carolyn Tate, at carolyn@carolyntate.co.

Disclaimer

Although the author and publisher have made every effort to ensure that the information in this book was correct at press time, the author and publisher do not assume and hereby disclaim any liability to any party for any loss, damage, or disruption caused by errors or omissions, whether such errors or omissions result from negligence, accident, or any other cause. All people and texts referenced in this book have been contacted for approval. If you have been quoted and overlooked providing permission, please contact the publisher.

The material in this publication is of the nature of general comment only and does not represent professional advice. It is not intended to provide specific guidance for particular circumstances and it should not be relied on as the basis for any decision to take action or not take action on any matter which it covers. Readers should obtain professional advice where appropriate before making any decision. To the maximum extent permitted by the law, the author and publisher disclaim all responsibility and liability to any person, arising directly from any person taking or not taking action based on information in this publication.

For more information visit carolyntate.co

Dedication

To the brave women who dare to write; may you find the courage to use your words to heal and serve.

Acknowledgement of Country

I acknowledge the Wurundjeri Woi Wurrung and Boon Wurrung people of the Kulin Nation who are the traditional owners of the land on which I live and write—and the great Birrarung River in which I swim. I pay my respects to elders past, present and emerging. I acknowledge these lands and waterways were never ceded and that it always was, and always will be, Aboriginal land.

Praise for Carolyn's Words and Work

Carolyn's love for nature and her ability to bring people together to learn, play and share is a beautiful gift. It has been a privilege to have numerous honest and meaningful conversations with her about loss, love and the future potential of ourselves and the natural world. —Loretta Bellato

Brave Women Write *is a manifesto for those who dare to write for healing and change—in your own life, in your community and for our world.* —Sara Clements

We need more women in the world like Carolyn, women with the courage to share their stories in service of helping others heal and grow. Combined with her belief in the power of purpose and of the written word, Carolyn's latest project will be a valuable resource for those looking to navigate through the complex times we find ourselves in with purpose and intent. —Deirdre Boyle

Carolyn is one of those rare humans who truly lives her values. Rather than avoiding difficulty or moving through too quickly, she listens deeply to all aspects of a narrative, not just the simple surface story and responds with compassion and courage. —Sieta Beckwith

Carolyn finds her heart in her writing and this is where she truly shines as she composes her thoughts based on real-life events. A truly inspirational teacher and mentor. —Gafiah Dickinson

Carolyn has an innate sense of awe and courage in both creative practices and her relationship to nature. She embodies the idea that true bravery involves testing yourself and finding comfort in discomfort. —Dr Meg Elkins

This book will help you write with more heart, truth and vulnerability. And it will make your everyday life more vibrant, purposeful and joyful. —Sarah Tovey

I love Carolyn's holistic and hands-on approach to helping people discover and articulate their purpose. She will meet you where you are at in your journey. Her frameworks and practices are simple, effective and accessible. Thanks Carolyn for your contribution to a more meaningful world. Please keep writing! —Nathalie Heynderickx

Carolyn's connection to nature and the Yarra Birrarung has helped heal her head, heart and hands. This book is a testament to the power of nature and how it can help us realise that we are capable of so much, if only we take a breath and trust in ourselves. —Charlotte Sterrett

This book will energise and inspire you to release your voice and share your stories with vulnerability, heart and hope. As a fledgling writer, I feel encouraged and supported to keep writing. I'm now more committed to picking up my pen again. Thank you! —Angela Raspass

Contents

Praise for Carolyn's Words and Work	5
With Love and Gratitude	9
Foreword by Carolyn Butler-Madden	11
Prologue *On Grief and Writing*	13
1. The End *On Naming Grief*	17
2. Returning Home *On Commitment*	23
3. Bead By Bead *On Goal-setting*	29
4. Glass Blinkers *On Routine*	35
5. A Room of One's Own *On Your Writing Space*	41
6. The Moment *On Knowing*	47
7. Your Story Matters *On Story-telling*	53
8. Interested and Interesting *On Story-catching*	59
9. Letting Go *On Story-releasing*	65
10. Freethinking Forebears *On Ancestral Elders*	69
11. Who's Your Heroine? *On Writing Icons*	75
12. Your Own Cheer-Squad *On Writers' Groups*	79
13. The Morning Pages *On Journaling*	85
14. A Balancing Act *On Life Practices*	91
15. Three Trees *On Knowledge*	97
16. The Brick Wall *On Courage and Recommitting*	103
17. Why? What? Who? *On Foundations*	107

18. And Now the *How* *On Planning*	113
19. My Top Seven *On Writing Skills*	117
20. Bring Your *Why* to Work *On Writing For Work*	123
21. The Quest Awaits *On The Hero's Journey*	129
22. A Woman's Quest *On The Heroine's Journey*	135
23. Kill the Good Girl *On Many Women's Stories*	141
24. Find Your Sister-tribe *On Community*	147
25. Find Your Sit-spot *On Mother Earth*	153
26. The Finish Line *On Facing Fear*	159
27. A Second Life *On Editing*	165
28. On the Shelf *On Publishing*	171
29. Making Waves *On Launching and Marketing*	177
30. Money, Money, Money *On Making a Living*	181
31. Remaking the World *On Movement-making*	185
32. Words to Write By *On Your Writer's Manifesto*	191
33. The End *On Endings and Beginnings*	195
Epilogue *Truth Be Known*	199
Recommended Reading	203
Other books by Carolyn Tate	205

With Love and Gratitude

It was grief that brought me to the page but it was my beloved writers' group that got me through this book. My heart is full of gratitude to Kath Walters, Yamini Naidu, Di Percy and Sandy McDonald for holding me in the grief and for the tough love. Without you spurring me on and challenging my self-doubt and procrastination, this book would not have seen the light of day.

Thank you to my son, Billy, for your unconditional love and support. You're the reason I write and never give up on it. If I can be some sort of example for you to pursue your purpose and be of service to others, I'll die happy.

To my mother, Joy Anear and sisters, Angela Bueti and Di Tate. Thank you for always listening and supporting me no matter what. Family means everything to me and you are the matriarch and the glue.

To Sara Clements and Sarah Tovey, thank you for being my first readers and providing such thoughtful feedback on how to improve this book. To my great friend, Angela Raspass, I am deeply grateful for your constant encouragement and words of wisdom on the final manuscript. To my design inspiration, Jacquie Swan. Your creativity is magic and so is our friendship.

To my brilliant publishing team; Roger McDonald, you're the kindest but most exacting editor I could hope for. Thanks for giving colour to my stories and making my words shine. Holly Dunn, thanks for your exquisite cover design. You have made this book stand out and make a statement. Michelle Pirovich, thanks for your thoughtful and diligent work in layout and design and getting the words onto the page. Marlene Rattigan, thanks for the proofreading and final magical polish up.

To the Yarra Birrarung river. Every day your waters helped heal my grief and find hope again. You gave me the courage to keep writing—and open my heart to love again.

Foreword
by Carolyn Butler-Madden

I love people who don't accept the status quo when it clearly isn't delivering the value it could or should.

Most people take the path well-trodden. They accept that this is how things are and they put their heads down and get on with it. But those who don't, often risk everything in search of a better way. Some succeed, some may not, but all have one thing in common. Courage. Courage that is driven by the belief that they must act.

Carolyn Tate is one of those people.

I first came across Carolyn as I embarked on my big career change from marketing to the world of purpose. When I published my first book in 2017, her name kept popping up. People kept asking me, 'do you know Carolyn Tate? If not, you need to.' Carolyn Tate was synonymous with purpose.

I then read her book *Conscious Marketing* and knew straight away I loved her; a woman seeking answers who was not prepared to settle for less. A woman of courage, whose search for meaning took her from a corporate career to Provence, to writing six books and becoming a pioneer of purpose—all underpinned by her personal purpose—to bring purpose to life so together we can build a better world.

We need more people of courage like Carolyn Tate. That's why I can't wait for this, her latest book, to get into the hands of people who are also on a search for greater meaning.

Carolyn's belief that it is women who will change the world, is one that I share. *Brave Women Write* is a manifesto for those women. It couldn't come at a more important time.

Carolyn Butler-Madden
Chief Purpose Activist, The Cause Effect

Prologue
On Grief and Writing

Grief. It's universal. We all experience it and we can't escape it, nor would we want to. It makes us fully human. It helps us become kinder, braver, better people. It leads us to a more meaningful life.

Many of us experience two levels of grief. The first is private grief: the death of a loved one, the end of a relationship, loss of work, pandemic-induced loneliness or the deep loss one feels when children leave the nest.

The second is a more ubiquitous, collective grief: a combination of rage and sorrow over the state of the world, the patriarchal systems that oppress women and minority groups, the unfathomable wars started by the world's sociopathic dictators, the lost voices and rights of our First Nation's people or the devastating destruction of Mother Earth.

There's no escaping grief in any and all its forms.

Yet grief is essential if we are to realise our greatness. Francis Weller's *The Wild Edge of Sorrow: Rituals of Renewal and the Scared Work of Grief* is a profound book on how to face grief and grow through it.

'Everyone must undertake an apprenticeship with sorrow. We must learn the art and craft of grief; discover the profound ways it ripens and deepens us. While grief is an intense emotion, it is also a skill we develop through a prolonged walk with loss. Facing grief is hard work. It takes outrageous courage to face outrageous loss. This is precisely what we are being called to do.'

My own grief was the catalyst for this book. It was caused by unrequited love and the end of my relationship—and the loss of hope for love.

Grief got me writing again after a six-month writing drought. And writing this book for you, got me through it. It was like an antidote, a challenging yet somehow miraculous cure for my heartbreak.

Brave Women Write is a book that will show you how to write with, and through, your grief. It's a selection of my own stories and the thirty-three practices I used to find hope again by getting my words down on the page and out into the world.

For me, writing is the most accessible and effective way to find relief from grief. It has the power to transform heartbreak into renewed hope—and even happiness. And if not happiness, at least a semblance of acceptance and reconciliation.

Writing is like a warm and comforting blanket. It's a place to wrap ourselves up, feel and express the grief, examine it and make sense of it in the scheme of our lives. Writing helps us move through, or at least accept the pain, so we can take action again.

And of course, writing is not just for dealing with grief and sorrow. It's for savouring pleasure too and for capturing the good times, the hope and the joy. It's for the precious moments of life to remind us why we're here, of our dreams and how we might make a better world.

Even if you're not experiencing grief right now, this book will still help you find your voice, get your words onto the page and your story written. You might just have decided that it's time to write your memoir. Or perhaps you want to make writing a practice for everyday life and become better at it. Or maybe you want to write an exposé and right some wrongs in your world. No matter, this book will still help you become a better, braver, bolder writer.

> **Brave words inspire brave deeds. And, in turn, brave deeds stimulate brave words.**

Many of us have dabbled in writing over the years but not made a commitment to it, as if it weren't essential to daily life but more a diversion to turn to if the mood strikes. We may, therefore, not yet have discovered its true potency and power for transformation.

When your writing originates from the purest source available to you, from your wild, courageous heart, it can transform your whole day. And if you can transform your day, you can transform your life. And if you can transform your life, you can transform the lives of those around you.

Brave women write, first for ourselves for private change, then for others for planetary change. We write words that are both meaningful to us and consequential for other women, for our communities and for the world beyond ourselves. We become activists with our words as we write (and work) towards a fair and just society for all.

Brave words inspire brave deeds. And, in turn, brave deeds stimulate brave words. The two go hand in hand. The world needs more brave women to write their stories, rewrite history and write her-story instead.

And we need more brave women doing brave deeds. Now, more than ever.

My aim is to help you free the writer within and show you how to make writing a practice for life.

In this book, I share the practices I use to face grief, find hope and write for personal and planetary change. Performed with purpose, the practices rewire your brain and rid you of any negative inner dialogue you might have around writing.

My aim is to help you free the writer within and show you how to make writing a practice for life.

If your plan is to write a book, *Brave Women Write* is the perfect guide to get you from big idea to published book. If your predilection is for other forms of writing such as poems, screenplays, blogs or even more journalistic news articles, this book will still help you develop practices to get your words down and out into the world.

However, I must warn that writing is a process and that your best laid plans (if you have any) might be best laid to rest. My advice is to be open and surrender to the process and see where it takes you. You might just end up producing something you had never dreamed of. Let creativity and curiosity take over.

To transform grief through writing, you must *do* the work of writing, not just read about the process. So, here's how I suggest you *do* this book:

- Commit to one practice per day over thirty-three days for thirty minutes per day
- Use a journal and pen and/or use a word document to capture notes and big ideas
- Complete the *Reflection and Action* exercises at the end of each practice
- As you read, formulate an idea for your writing project, set a goal and begin.

If you need company to get through your writing project, find a writing buddy or start a writers' group. All it takes is a friend or two with the will and courage to get writing with you—and to share their grief and stories.

My own writers' group is the reason this book is in your hands now and it's why I recommend starting your own. You'll find a chapter on writers' groups in these pages and a guide on how to start and run your own group on my website. Just click on the QR code on the inside cover and share it with your writer friends.

I hope *Brave Women Write* becomes an essential companion to help you write throughout your life, your loss and your grief towards hope and joy. Onwards!

Reflection and Action

Why are you embarking on *Brave Women Write*?
What do you hope to gain from it?

1. The End
On Naming Grief

It's January 2000 and I'm thirty-six. I'm on the final leg of a long run. Sprinting around the final corner, I stop at the peak of the hill to catch my breath. Looking down the hill, just one hundred metres away, my beautiful home is waiting for me. Inside that beautiful home is my loyal, generous husband and my sweet, cheerful two-year-old son.

My mind goes into over-drive.

It's early Saturday evening. I should be happy and on a high after this run before settling in for a pleasant evening with my family with nowhere to go and nothing to do. I'm not though. I'm dreading going home. I just don't think I can do this any longer.

My breath returns and I prepare for the sprint home. Nothing. My legs won't move. I collapse on my backside in the gutter. Gut-wrenching sobs reverberate throughout my whole body. I'm scared by their intensity. Sometime later, I somehow muster up the energy to rise and plod those final steps home.

Heart-in-mouth, I walk in the front door and deliver the excruciating truth to my husband. 'I'm not happy. I can't do this anymore,' I say. It's the death knell on our marriage.

What ensues over the next twelve months is a kind of protracted heartbreak for the both of us, as we agree amicably to end our twenty-year relationship.

But why? What was wrong with me? I was the quintessential modern woman with everything I could seemingly want: a wonderful husband, reasonable brains and beauty, good health, a gorgeous son, a well-paying corporate job, a stunning home, plenty of money for holidays, clothes and entertainment, lots of fabulous friends and a loving family.

Life was extremely comfortable. On the outside, to others, I no doubt appeared happy, content and successful. On the inside, however, I felt numb and trapped. Something big was missing from my life.

> **We don't free ourselves because with freedom comes uncertainty and self-responsibility and most of us find these extremely frightening. It's safer to stay in gaol.**

Pause and ponder now. I'm fully aware that my story may read like a cliché, a hackneyed version of many other privileged white women's stories. Perhaps this has been you. Or perhaps you've read various iterations of the same story of other women. Clichés are, in fact, truisms. Take the overworked story and dig into it. What is it telling you? Clichés exist for a reason. They make us wince because they are agonisingly true.

I first read this well-known story in Lori Gottlieb's book, *Maybe You Should Talk to Someone*. It portrays a prisoner trapped behind the bars of a gaol cell. She shakes the bars desperately trying to get out but to her right and left the cell is open—no bars. All she has to do is walk around but still she frantically shakes the bars.

That was me. And I suspect it's true for many women at times. We feel completely stuck, trapped in our life or situation, unable to see a way out from behind the bars. We become imprisoned by our beliefs, roles, relationships, fears and the stories we tell about ourselves.

We imprison ourselves because it's more comfortable behind the bars. We don't free ourselves because with freedom comes uncertainty and self-responsibility and most of us find these extremely frightening. It's safer to stay in gaol.

And it becomes an insidious, unacknowledged and, therefore, unexamined form of grief while our inner fire slowly dies.

From birth, like many women of my day, my path had been preordained. Gender conditioning was unrecognised and, therefore, unquestioned. The 'good girl' grew up to be the 'dutiful woman'. I was the role-model daughter and student who then became the role-model employee, wife, mother and housekeeper.

These roles had become my bars.

For years, I'd suppressed a growing sense of dissatisfaction. I'd pushed it down, barely admitting it to myself let alone my husband, mother, sisters or a trusted girlfriend. I bore the brunt of my unhappiness alone and it was a heavy cross to bear.

One day with a friend, a year before the beginning of the end, we'd come across a tarot reader at a shop selling services of a spiritual nature. She was eager to have a reading for a bit of fun—and she did. Not me. I was so paranoid it would reveal the truth of my unhappiness that I refused outright. I was prepared to go to any lengths to suppress my true feelings.

I know now that it wasn't just that I was no longer in love with my husband who, by the way, was just as 'dutiful' as I was. It was because I knew there was something more for me other than a lifetime of marriage, motherhood and working for 'the man'. I had no idea who I really was, what truly mattered to me or what gifts I had to offer the world.

I was also deeply ashamed that I was unhappy, given all that I possessed. Why wasn't I just grateful? Why couldn't I just 'shut up and put up' and get on with life? Things were not that bad.

Not. That. Bad.

I suspect these three tiny words keep so many women from living their best life.

Most of us get stuck behind the bars at various times in our life. Sometimes the bars are so heavy we stop shaking them and retreat. We descend into resignation and depression. We let them defeat us. Sometimes the bars are not so heavy. We can see right through them towards freedom on the other side but life's 'not that bad' so we only shake them intermittently. We half accept them, and half detest them, and do nothing about them.

At other times, like me, we reach a point where we've simply had enough. We won't put up with the bars any longer and in a single moment of clarity and courage we take a step sideways and forwards into uncharted territory.

The bars appear time and again in our lives and their nature differs for every woman. For me it was all the roles I was playing preventing me from truly knowing myself. For others it might be more specifically to do with work, money, culture, religion, sex, family circumstances or relationships. Recognising exactly what keeps us trapped is the first step towards personal freedom.

> **Not. That. Bad.**
> **I suspect these three tiny words keep so many women from living their best life.**

The story of the bars that imprison us is not just pertinent to each of us as women. It's pertinent to all women. Women everywhere recognise a deep, collective rage and sorrow that we're still pinned behind the man-made bars; that we live in a world that continues to oppress and desecrate women. According to the *2020 World Economic Forum Global Gender Gap* research, it will be another ninety-nine years before we close the gender gap. While we're making progress, it often feels hopelessly drawn-out to me.

I believe it's impossible to become an activist for the women of the world if we're not activists in our own private lives. We must step out of our own gaols so we can inspire and support other women to step out of theirs.

After the end of my marriage, I transitioned into a new life. I moved into a new home, became a single mother and quit my corporate job to start my own business. I made a commitment to build a new life on what mattered to me and not what our patriarchal society had conditioned me for.

> **It's impossible to become an activist for the women of the world if we're not activists in our own private lives.**

While I was relieved at my new-found liberation, I didn't just thoughtlessly move on. Accompanying my gaolbreak was my first real heartbreak because my husband was my first real love. So, one moment I'd be filled with hope and happiness. The next I'd be filled with grief and regret. It was a weird blend of emotions, equal parts oil and water, the two never mixing yet uncomfortably co-existing.

I didn't have writing in my life at the time to help me make sense of it all. I wasn't aware that I could transform my grief into healing and gold through the written word. Now, some twenty years later, I can see how helpful and transformative it might have been.

Without this radical life-change, however, I would not have discovered my love of writing some six years later. I would not have found either the curiosity or the courage to unleash my creativity if I'd remained behind the bars. 'This, I know for sure,' as Oprah would say.

And I would not be writing right now without my most recent heartbreak over the end of romantic love. Grief brought me to the page and this book is the way to navigate my way through.

I've learnt that grief and love are inexplicably intertwined. We can't fully love if we've never fully experienced grief. And we can't fully experience grief if we've never fully loved. So, I suppose a life well-lived is always going to be marred with grief. Therefore, we must learn how to accept and live with sorrow, just as we do with joy.

To face grief, we must first name it, whether it's personal and private grief or universal grief over world affairs beyond our control. To befriend it, we must understand its source so we can examine it and make sense of it. No matter the source, writing is the pathway through to hope and positive action.

Reflection and Action

Name your grief and write about it.
How will writing help you face it?

2. Returning Home
On Commitment

More than 220,000 words. That's how many I wrote in the year the world went dark. Words in journals, blogs and three half-finished non-fiction manuscripts. Writing was my anchor in the annus horribilis of 2020. It kept me mostly sane and steady throughout the almost interminable Melbourne lockdowns.

Around the end of the lockdown in November 2020, I abruptly stopped writing. It was a response to being free to re-engage with life outside my four walls again, the need to refocus on my business after the impact of COVID—and the ending (once and for all) of my love relationship.

Six months passed. Not one word written. Nothing. I wondered if I was depressed. I wasn't certain, the Black Dog never having savaged me before. But there was an invisible, oppressive cloak of joylessness about me on the outside. And a sad streak running from head to toe on the inside.

I was trying to make sense of the end of love while still clinging to the idea there might be a future for us. It was an *ending*, but not really the *end*, at least in my own heart and mind. I wasn't yet struck by intense grief, just stuck in a kind of futile, stagnant, unhappy hope.

And I was frustrated at failing to finish even one of the manuscripts I'd started. I'd written and published five books before. I knew I had it in me. So why had I written in circles, jumping from one project to the next, scarcely writing a jot nor bringing any of the books to fruition?

I was wordless and loveless. Empty.

I tried therapy. I tried immersing myself in nature. I tried yoga, swimming, dancing, running, eating healthily, eliminating alcohol, seeking guidance from my sisters, girlfriends and my poor long-suffering son. I tried everything to find my writing mojo again.

Everything. Except writing.

On one restless and sleepless night, I began agonising over it. I wondered whether I was serious about pursuing the writer's life I'd imagined for myself for many years. The next morning, I rummaged through my keepsake box and pulled out the commitment statement I'd created on a writing sabbatical in Aix-en-Provence, France, in 2010. It's handwritten on bright yellow card in my best cursive script and adorned with clear glass crystals and a red velvet love-heart.

In France, I'd produced the manuscript for *Unstuck in Provence*, with Julia Cameron's *The Artist's Way* as my constant companion. Before getting started, she'd insisted readers create their own statement. Miraculously, it seemed to work. It saw me through to the end of the first draft. And years later it provided the encouragement I needed to finish and publish two subsequent books.

Could it now re-inspire me to become a finisher (and a fighter) again?

If you're committed to making writing a life practice, I highly recommend producing a commitment statement and showcasing it prominently on your desk. It will be there in the good times—and the bad. It should not fail you.

Yet it might, if you just throw it in a keepsake box and ignore it, as I had. It will disappoint you if you neglect to do the work of writing. Because doing the work is the only thing that matters. Showing up at the blank page, day-in and day-out to write, even if you have zero inspiration, is the only path to healing grief and becoming a better, braver writer. It's the only work to be done. Through you, and by you.

Great advice to myself that I had not taken for too long now.

An old saying declares, 'We teach what we most need to learn'. I've found it's much the same for writing. We most often write what we most need to learn. Such sweet irony.

Here's my commitment statement. Food for thought to write your own.

I, Carolyn Tate, am a brilliant, prolific and respected writer and author. My creativity heals me and my readers and leads me to truth and love. I live and work globally, while earning an excellent income from my writing.

Reading it slowly, attempting to make meaning of every word, it suddenly felt like nonsense. A sad fabrication. A lie. Sure, I'd been a prolific writer during lockdown, but I was no longer writing. And I'd not published one book in the last four years. I could no longer claim to be an author—certainly not a recent one.

Angry at myself and tempted to rip it up, I eventually calmed down with a cup of chai and chose instead to be kind to myself, reflect on the declaration and assess the possibility of recommitting to it.

Was I serious about my craft? Or was I a mere dabbler? There's nothing wrong with dabbling per se. In fact, it's important when you first start to get a sense of things, a feel for your writing, to determine if it's yours to keep. But, if you dabble too much and don't devote time to it, I guarantee it will result in frustration, feelings of uselessness and ultimate abandonment.

It's much like the person you love who is a dilettante, never committing. You know deep down they're trifling with the relationship. I knew it for more than three long years. Blind love is the worst kind. But I digress.

If you've been a long-term tinkerer and haven't wholeheartedly loved your writing, it won't love you back. It knows when you've accepted the self-doubt, the convenient diversions, the excuses of time constraints or the unreasonable demands of your boss or your family as reasons for not writing. You've put everything and everyone else before your words. Why would they love you back?

For healing is the first great purpose of writing. It brings you back to truth and love. It will be with you when you can't be with yourself. It won't lie to you.

There comes a point where you must stop doodling and commit to writing. You make it a practice, not necessarily your life's work but something to give your undivided attention to on a very regular basis, preferably daily. And that's where your commitment statement comes in handy. It's a constant reminder to keep producing.

In an instant, that same morning, I decided to recommit myself to my craft, to make that statement as real and meaningful as I'd intended it to be on the day I first penned it.

The decision made, I now had to determine which of the unfinished works lying around in that dark, cavernous file marked 'Current Manuscripts' would be first to win my approval for publication. Which one called me loudest, if any? Each of the unfinished manuscripts contained many stories I was fond of. How could I possibly choose one narrative over another?

That night an idea took a hold. Its origin remains a mystery. Creativity is like that. Ideas find you, you don't find them. But beware the perils of ignoring or failing to capture an idea that visits you from some unidentifiable, cosmic source. It will promptly bid you farewell and search for another more welcoming host. Then one day you'll discover this other human had found the courage to run with it. They'll have shared your idea with the world and you'll be left bewildered and bereft wondering why you turned your back on it.

My idea was to write a different book all together, one that would include the very best stories from each of the unfinished manuscripts. I envisioned a book of reflections and the lessons I've learned about storytelling and writing and how to use them for healing and transformation.

For healing is the first great purpose of writing. It brings you back to truth and love. It will be with you when you can't be with yourself. It won't lie to you.

Some days later I'd still not found the courage to begin pouring over the manuscripts to select the stories and begin rewriting. For five days I arose at six in the morning to get started. For five days nothing came. I sat at my laptop numb, blocked and wordless, petrified I'd lost the will to write forever.

> **I'd found my way back to writing and it had found its way back to me.**

And then on the afternoon of that fifth day, a Friday, the perfect storm occurred. It was a moment of great import—a conversation with *him* over a long walk in the park after a six-month exile. It was an encounter I'd initiated and he'd somewhat reluctantly agreed to.

'I do not love you,' he said kindly yet firmly looking directly into my eyes. 'I won't come back again. Every time I do, I will myself to jump into the abyss of love with you but something holds me back. I won't hurt you anymore.' They were the words he'd not had the courage to express at the end of 2020 and the very words I needed to hear.

And as if this was not enough, he added the final insult to injury. 'And I have met someone else.' It really was the end this time. Nothing kills hope faster than learning your ex has moved on to a new lover.

What followed was one of the angriest and saddest two weeks of my life. It was a soul-destroying, crushing period of deep mourning and letting go. I have only my sisters, friends and son to thank for supporting me through it. Then one Monday morning, feeling washed up and wrung out, yet now surrendered, calm and clear, I arose to attempt to write again.

This time the words flowed.

I'd found my way back to writing and it had found its way back to me.

Reflection and Action

Write your own commitment statement for your writing practice.

3. Bead By Bead
On Goal-setting

Choosing which stories to share would always be tough. I had more than seventy stories across three different manuscripts on themes from activism to feminism and community-building to consider. I had no criteria for selection or rejection but I knew that only a third were likely to make the grade.

Would I start with a stock-take, lining them all up against each other, prodding and poking them to assess their worth? Did they even have a place in the same book? How were they relevant to each other and how would they flow seamlessly from one to the next? What if I chose the weak candidates and neglected the champions? And, of course, what did any of them have to do with grief and writing?

Far too many questions. Absolutely no answers.

My friend and writers' group buddy, Kath Walters, is a superb book coach and the author of *Overnight Authority*. She helps businesspeople write business books in ninety days following a clear and proven process. She focuses with a steely eye on structure and finishing. Kath is the consummate finisher; she is the completion queen. I, too, used a clear process like Kath's for my last two books and I'd established the same process for my half-finished manuscripts.

The process for business books usually works like this:

Start by clearly identifying who you are writing for—your audience. Determine the specific question the book answers or the problem it solves for them. Then produce a table of contents and chapter outline ensuring each chapter addresses a specific element of the question or problem. Each chapter should include research and evidence to support your case and a story to bring the whole point of the chapter to life.

Ensure your book has a powerful opening story, a neat conclusion to wrap it all up and a cadence to it that helps readers make logical progress towards the ultimate solution to their problem. It might also pose some questions to the reader, offer exercises to complete or a neat summary of the main points at the end of each chapter.

The final step is to set a word target—by chapter and for the whole book. And then it's down to work. Time to write.

If you're just starting out, this formula might be a good one to follow. It will help you create a system to get the work done. This is the only thing that matters if you're committed to freeing the writer within. Find a system that works for you and then do the work of writing. Get the words out on the page, no matter how awful you believe them to be. Your goal is to take a leaf out of Kath's book—to be a finisher.

> **Bead by bead, I'd thread this book together and mend my broken heart.**

So, the big question for this book became: would this process work for me? Rationally it could work but my heart rejected it. I couldn't fathom the idea of getting stuck in the heady process of setting a structure then poring through the pages of old manuscripts to find the right stories to fit before actually writing anything.

That's when I recalled this charming quote by Brenda Ueland, author of the 1938 classic on the art of authorship *If You Want to Write: A Book about Art, Independence and Spirit.*

She writes, 'I learned that you should feel when writing, not like Lord Byron on a mountain top, but like a child stringing beads in kindergarten—happy, absorbed and quietly putting one bead on after another.'

That's what I'd be. A child again. Choose one bead or story. Thread it with my full attention. Then choose another. And the next. And the next. I'd choose the story that spoke to me most each morning, not planning which would come next. It would be a story that would be most healing for my grief and bring me most relief that day. Bead by bead, I'd thread this book together and mend my broken heart. It was thrilling to know I'd have a brand-new adventure each day, retrieving then refreshing each tale and finding new lessons in each.

It was a very different approach for me, unlike anything I'd ever followed before.

Regardless of your writing predilection (journaling, books, blogs, poems, songs, screenplays), you'll do this too as your creative prowess improves. When you first start to write, it makes sense to follow the colour-by-numbers process.

But the more you write, the more your confidence will grow. You'll want to break the rules and start venturing off-piste. Over the years, you'll progress from beginner skier to mastery of the black-run slopes and finally you'll start to create your own ski trails. You'll begin to write following a process that is uniquely yours. And you may even begin to expand into new writing territory from books to poems to songs and so on.

For *Brave Women Write*, there was only one rule, however, one discipline I had to apply if my approach was to work. That was the imperative of finishing according to Kath's edict—to have the first-draft manuscript completed in ninety days. I could not bear the thought of ending up with yet another half-baked tome lying dormant in that dark cavern of my computer, forgotten and unpublished.

So, I set myself a goal to complete a sixty thousand word manuscript in ninety days.

That was it. My first goal was simply to complete the first draft. I didn't think about the second or third drafts, who would edit it, design the cover or format the layout. I refused to contemplate how, or with whom, I would be published. I avoided dreaming about the book launch celebrations, the outfit I'd wear or the standing ovation I might receive at my triumphant speech. I did not speculate on whether the book would be a blockbuster or an embarrassing flop.

My only thought was of finishing the first-draft, a complete manuscript where I would euphorically type The End on my ninety-day D-day.

Goals are necessary if you intend sharing your work with the world. If not, don't worry. Just keep playing and creating and relish the exquisite goal-lessness of it all. Devote yourself to your writing for your own private healing purposes and pay no further heed to this.

Goals give us hope and focus and help us access that sweet state of flow, which is where the magic happens.

But if you do intend to unleash your work on the public (which I recommend because if it helps just one other person you will have committed a mighty deed), you must have a goal. Not a goal to become an international best-selling author speaking to adoring audiences all over the world but a goal to just write and get the first draft done. In the process, at the very least, you will have helped and healed yourself.

> **That's what writing does. It helps you tease out the lessons from the events of your life. And it helps you make wiser choices in the future. It helps you let go, move on and create new dreams.**

Do not focus on your 'Zero to Hero' dream just yet, a dream that takes you from non-author to Booker Prize winner or from rags to riches like J.K. Rowling with the Harry Potter series. It will kill your creativity and put that commitment statement at risk of mockery and ultimate abandonment.

You need your first goal to be do-able, something to keep you focused for the immediate and foreseeable future. Word by word. Chapter by chapter. Day by day. Week by week. Month by month. A maximum of one year, no longer. If you detect a sense of repetition in these last lines, you're alive to the secret of writing. It's all about rhythm and routine.

You need a goal that takes you from shaky ground to the first solid step. As Martin Luther King once said, 'you don't have to see the whole staircase to take the first step'. That's what you need to do. Find your courage and just take the first step.

Perhaps this is more like it?

'You don't have to see the whole necklace to thread the first bead.' That's certainly a worse maxim than Martin Luther King's, but it was worth it to feel your reaction, your cringe, your intelligence needled. Words do that. They divide us and annoy us. They make our hearts and minds either shrink or expand. Woe betide the words that do neither.

Goals, intentions or dreams (call them what you will) are vital for moving forward with your writing—and in life, of course. Goals give us hope and focus and help us access that sweet state of flow, which is where the magic happens. Once you set your writing goal and get started on it, pay attention, notice how the flow feels.

Shared goals are also what make a relationship flourish. I see clearly now there were no common goals in my own love affair. It seemed to me that for him, our relationship was a week by week proposition, directly opposed to my hopes for our unification. I wanted to plan adventures and share more of our lives. I wanted 'us' to evolve, to create plans for our future. It was a constant source of angst and frustration for me.

I couldn't express my hopes and needs in a mature way and instead would retreat into silence and sadness. This would result in bursts of anger at him and me ultimately calling an end to the relationship, which he would accept without a fight, until I'd get lonely and reel him back in again. And the pattern went on for more than three long years.

Most of the time we did spend together, however, was deliciously vital and tender in so many ways. Before meeting him, for more than three long years my heart had been shut tight to love and he had cracked it open again. I am grateful, not to him, but to myself for taking the risk to love.

It's excruciatingly embarrassing to write this, yet it feels true to me. One would think that by the ripe old age of fifty-something, I'd have it all worked out. Yet here I am still learning—about relationships and myself. That's what writing does. It helps you tease out the lessons from the events of your life. And it helps you make wiser choices in the future. It helps you let go, move on and create new dreams. We are never too old to learn.

In the end, perhaps we did a share a goal—to cease our harmful patterns once and for all so we'd both be free to seek a greater love than we could ever give each other.

What's calling out to you to be written? Whatever it is, set a goal and get writing.

Reflection and Action
What are you writing and what's your goal?

4. Glass Blinkers
On Routine

With a goal set to write a sixty thousand word manuscript in ninety days, I chose to break this book into thirty-three chapters, each no longer than two thousand words. I'd write three chapters a week or about five thousand words per week over twelve weeks from Monday to Friday from seven to ten in the morning at a minimum. That would give me a complete manuscript and a decent sized book of two hundred plus pages.

No matter what you're writing, break your goal into small daily or weekly targets. A target helps you gain momentum and get the words out. The more consistent you are in producing your text, the greater the cumulative healing. It's akin to daily or weekly therapy.

To achieve your writing goal, however, you need a routine. This routine, after a time, will become a habit. And before you know it, writing becomes an indelible part of your life. It becomes a daily practice essential for your wellbeing, as vital as exercise and a healthy diet.

With targets set, it's time to prepare yourself for the act of writing. I'm not one who can just jump out of bed and open my laptop bleary-eyed to write. I must prepare myself. Each morning upon waking, I journal in bed before a walk or swim and shower.

Then before starting work, I make a coffee, put on some music, light a candle and set my writing intentions for the morning. Contemporary, classical or devotional music is the best accompaniment for me. I can't write to lyrics as they're too distracting so it must be instrumental music. It offers the most direct access to my heart and creative vein. That reminds me of the words of Ernest Hemingway (and others), 'There's nothing to writing. All you do is sit down at a typewriter and bleed.' That's what music does—it pierces my aorta so I can bleed words. Not such a pretty image. Sorry.

I don't just then sit for three hours solid and write. I set the timer for one hour. When it goes off, I arise for a five-minute break for five salutes to the sun, a dance around the table or a bowl of porridge, whatever takes my fancy. I then return to my desk and take ten long deep breaths. Inhalation. Exhalation. Inspiration. Then I get back to work for another hour, do it again and then one final hour. I do not allow emails, phone calls, work or friends to divert me from my mission.

To get the work done, you must have a routine that works for you, your lifestyle, family and work commitments. You might be a morning person, a late-night person and/or a weekend person. Whatever it is, make the space in your day or week, even if it's just fifteen minutes in the morning and fifteen at night. Commit to filling that space with your heavenly heart-healing words. Make it the only thing that matters—at least while you're doing it. No distractions. Non-negotiable.

Play around with various ways to make the most of your precious writing time. Try the Pomodoro technique (twenty-five minutes of writing undisturbed, a five-minute break, twenty-five minutes of writing again and so on). Google it and give it a go. Or just set a timer for a period that works for you. Turn off all social media and notifications. Put up a 'Do Not Disturb' sign on your door. Commit to not getting out of your chair until the timer goes off. Or commit to not moving until you've reached your word target. One hundred words. Five hundred words. One thousand words.

Ensure you include mini-breaks to keep the energy flowing and get creative with how you use them. Fifty star-jumps. AC/DC at one hundred decibels. A run around the block. And make sure it's not digital; social media is the worst way to fill a break. Make it physical, activities that get your face smiling, your body moving and your heart racing. And then get back to work.

> **Mother Nature is always my greatest escape. She somehow knows what's ailing me and helps me navigate my way through and out the other side.**

One morning, after a few days of writing, I jumped into my story-bank to go hunting for my next treasure. Five minutes later, I'd happily chosen a story. After an hour of toying with it I became blocked and frustrated. My story wasn't going anywhere. It just didn't seem to fit. I couldn't make it work.

Writing will do that. It's like your most precious toddler. He brings you much delight one moment and in the next he's in such a tantrum you'd willingly adopt him out.

That's when I broke a principal rule. I gave up.

I pushed myself away from the desk, pulled on my puffer jacket and runners and trudged down the street to walk by the great Birrarung Marr. On Wurundjeri Woi Wurrung Country, 'Birrarung' is the traditional name of the Yarra River while 'marr' refers to the mist that sometimes settles over the river. Loosely, the words are often translated to 'river of mists'.

> **Blocks, when accepted and treated with great kindness, will always precipitate exquisite bouts of courage and creative brilliance.**

Mother Nature is always my greatest escape. She somehow knows what's ailing me and helps me navigate my way through and out the other side. After only five minutes, she delivered and helped me identify the two major reasons for my block.

First was the relationship—not surprisingly. An unwelcome feeling that I could only identify as resentment had stealthily crept up on me overnight. It was like a gargantuan black stone sitting in my heart. It was to do with my greatest purpose of authorship. In the three years prior to meeting him, I'd published three books, yet in the three plus years we'd been whirling in and out of each other's lives, I'd not published one. I'd bestowed so much energy on him and the possibility of 'us' that I'd neglected to pursue my purpose to produce and publish books.

That's what a relationship with the wrong person will do. Instead of it firing up and fuelling your purpose, it will unwittingly subvert, divert and even destroy it. And that's what had happened for me. It was not his fault. It was mine. I just couldn't see it at the time.

I had to remove that black stone before I could return to my desk and write something worthy. I was consumed by an onslaught of angry, sad, repetitive thoughts and feelings. Not one thought was left unturned or unexamined. It was harrowing but necessary if I was to process and release it. For immovable resentment is like a form of incurable cancer.

My dear friend, Deb Rayner, had taught me how to use Emotional Freedom Techniques (EFT) or physical tapping on my body's energy meridians to work through and release painful feelings. So, I tapped and cried, and cried and tapped some more. For how long, I can't be sure. Yet somehow it worked. The black stone became a small, smooth rose-quartz crystal.

When that was done, I turned my attention to the second reason for my block. I was fretting over the possibility that my plan was flawed, that my story-bank tales would simply not work. Attempting to retrofit them to an entirely different work seemed lazy, even disingenuous. If this was the book I must write, perhaps I'd have to let my old stories go and start all over again.

What to do? Standing on a river bridge, face to the sun, an idea occurred. What if I was to perform a complete about-turn? Instead of finding the story first then trying to make a lesson out of it, what if I decided on the lesson and let that drive the story? Perhaps that story could be one from my existing story-bank or an entirely new one? Why limit myself? And why, dear reader, would you even have to know? A writer, like a magician, is not obliged to reveal her bag of tricks to anyone.

That was it! I gave myself full license to change tack, to write unfettered for complete creative freedom.

I almost sprinted home. I couldn't wait to slide into my chair and get onto my laptop. With these two blocks gone, the words flowed.

> You must also give yourself full permission to change tack to get the job done.

That hoary old chestnut, the writer's block: it happens to everyone. Maybe your head is full of junky, unhelpful thoughts leaving no space for the words to flow. Or perhaps the process you're following simply doesn't work, no matter which way you try to manipulate it. Or it could be you're exhausted, depressed or devoid of creative inspiration and you just can't face writing that day.

When blocks happen, and they will occur often, accept them with grace and self-compassion. Don't beat yourself up about it. If you do, you'll only add more pain to an already difficult experience. Instead, approach the block with composure.

'Ah, there you are,' you might say to yourself with a wry smile. Acknowledge it. Accept it. Then act on it. You must have a circuit-breaker up your sleeve, a way to solve the problem that's preventing you from doing the work—a way that will have you returning to your desk with determination rather than despair. It could be a solo hike in the mountains, a boozy lunch with your writers' group, a power nap or a deep night's sleep. For me, it's always a long, solo commune with Mother Nature. She never fails me.

Blocks, when accepted and treated with great kindness, will always precipitate exquisite bouts of courage and creative brilliance. They will lead you to an even deeper truth. Learn to love them and trust that on the other side lies the answer you seek.

You must also give yourself full permission to change tack to get the job done. Turn your sails away from the direction in which you were heading. Take a small diversion or chart an entirely new course if you must. Adhering to the notion that the first way is the only way will kill your creativity. Whatever you do though, don't stop creating.

My friend, Angela Raspass, urges her clients to wear 'glass blinkers' when pursuing a goal. I love that. Glass blinkers allow you to focus on the track ahead while offering peripheral vision so you can correct course if needed. Glass blinkers keep you connected to your routine and they get you to the finish line.

Once you've broken down your goal into daily or weekly targets, experiment with your routine to discover what works best for you. When to write. How often to write. When to take breaks. How to deal with blocks.

It will take you a while to discover your own unique regimen. No-one else's routine will suit you. It must be yours and yours alone. I promise you, as incongruous as it may seem, that a routine is the direct path to creative liberation—and healing your grief.

Reflection and Action
What writing routines will you experiment
with and adopt?

5. A Room of One's Own
On Your Writing Space

'A woman must have money and a room of her own if she is to write fiction,' declares Virginia Woolf in the 1929 essay *A Room of One's Own*. Her essay argues for both a literal and figurative space for women to write in a literary world dominated by men.

Woolf was fortunate to have both money and a room of her own so she could devote herself to writing. Perhaps you don't have the means (yet) to make writing your single obsession. You must, however, have a room of your very own. Or, at the very least, your own space and a desk of your own. You must have a private zone where the real world is left behind so you can transport yourself into another realm.

In Aix-en-Provence, in 2010, ten years after my divorce, I first understood the necessity of having my own writer's space. Incidentally, it was also where I first understood the imperative of writing as the way to heal grief. Another heartbreak had precipitated that sojourn and inspired *Unstuck in Provence*. Sorry, you'll have to read the book if you want to know more. My grief over that relationship has long since died; powerful evidence that writing is the way.

At the time, I'd sold our home in Sydney, culled most of our belongings and set up a rental home in Melbourne before taking off. It was liberating owning very little and owing nothing. I was free of the burdens of debt, material stuff and the need to earn a living from meaningless yet well-paid work for six months. It was a priceless, albeit high-risk, opportunity to experience a full-time writer's life and a priceless opportunity for my son, Billy, to experience an education in a new country.

The moment we stepped over the threshold of our pocket-sized rental apartment on the fourth floor of an eighteenth century building remains etched in my memory. It was instant love. We had a bedroom for me and a cosy loft with a bed for Billy overlooking the open-plan living area. Wooden beams covered in evergreen vines extended across the gabled roof and the whole apartment was filled with an ethereal, natural light.

The pièce de résistance was the three hundred and sixty degree views over Aix and Mont Sainte-Victoire from the rooftop garden. It was the minutest and sweetest burrow any writer could wish for.

> **You must have a private zone where the real world is left behind so you can transport yourself into another realm.**

The corner of the living room under the stairs held a small desk. It was a rather tired crimson-red laminate affair, nothing flash at all and something you'd likely toss out for your next hard-rubbish collection. Yet it was mine alone upon which I'd create unencumbered. It became affectionately known as my 'little red writers' desk'.

On one corner of the desk sat my commitment statement and a purple card upon which I'd written my writing goal and weekly plan. Each day I'd add an item for inspiration: a vintage postcard from the local markets, the birthday card from Billy, and in the final days before typing The End, a small bottle of Moët. Throughout this time, *The Artist's Way* sat right beside me, a constant companion willing me to keep going.

I'd positioned the desk so I could stare out the window for stimulation when stuck for words. When taking a break, I'd fling it open to peer down on the townsfolk in the public square below and tune into their mellifluous voices floating through the air. At dusk, as Billy was supposedly doing his homework, I'd retreat to the rooftop with an aperitif, a reward for achieving the day's word count.

My little red writers' desk was the workbench for a good eighty percent of *Unstuck in Provence*. I wrote the balance at the local English bookshop and café, *Book in Bar*, an exquisite little hidey-hole in which I drank far too much black coffee and occasionally connected with other hopeful authors.

Many times during this writing retreat, I'd glance up to survey the apartment and pinch myself at the surrealism of it all. I'd reflect on the simple, creative life we were living, and a sense of pure joy and contentment would suffuse me. Almost daily I'd vow to emulate this life on our return to Melbourne. Meaning would become my new money. Writing would be my world. I'd live an artist's existence and reject the material life.

I'm guessing you already know where this story is going.

Back in Melbourne in 2011, I promptly forgot my vow. Within six months, I'd bought a new house for Billy and me in an inner-city suburb. In no time, I filled it with just as many possessions as we'd had in Sydney. Then, of course, there was debt, a new car, renovations and the stress of needing to earn a living to pay for it all through means other than writing. I'd become an unconscious consumer again with nary a backwards glance at the free life we'd lived in France.

Despite this, the will to write remained strong. I set up my own snug writing lair in the corner of the garage which had been renovated into an office with a lovely desk, comfy chair and bookshelf filled with my favourite classics. On the desk, sat my commitment statement, a few small paintings, cards from friends, a candle and books and papers piled high. It came together handsomely, even if it wasn't quite like the south of France.

You can do this too, no matter where you live. Find a room of your own, a space of your own at home, a tiny corner in which to create. Make it yours alone. Make it off-limits to others. Make it so gorgeously enticing that you can't wait to get out of bed and get to work in it.

If there's no room at home or too many distractions to contend with from other humans, look elsewhere. Perhaps you have a family member or neighbour with a spare room or attic to set up as your writing escape or a fellow writer or artist willing to offer you a desk in their creative space. Or perhaps you'll find a community of writers and artists in your town with space to rent.

Designing your own creative nest is a fabulously joyful exercise.

One of the benefits of having writing as your artistic pursuit is that you can engage in it anywhere. All you need is a laptop and access to the internet. While I can write in hotels, shared office-spaces and cafés if I must, there is nothing quite like my desk at home. It both stimulates and goads me to do the work, day after day. Over time you'll learn to write anywhere too but when you're starting out, there's nothing like a space of your own.

Today, Billy is no longer that twelve-year-old boy. He's a mature adult and living life his way in his own place. And I no longer live in that home that eventually became too big, too cumbersome and too much to manage for a woman alone. I sold up again to downsize and minimalise so I could give myself the best possible chance of returning to the vow I'd made in France.

In August 2018, I moved into my newly-built small-footprint apartment within a community of like-minded creatives, academics and professionals. It was the very same size as that French apartment yet in a city-fringe northern suburb still in my beloved city, Melbourne.

So now nothing could stop me from devoting myself to my plan of becoming a prolific author. Or could it?

'Life is what happens to you, when you're busy making other plans,' John Lennon wrote.

We'd already known each other for twelve months, when he slept with me on a makeshift bed on the first night in my new apartment. Together we created a vision of how this unfilled space would become a heavenly home. Being a successful theatre designer, he had the know-how and the talent while I had the willingness and the wallet (albeit a modest one) for the vision to become a reality.

In weeks, we'd transformed my home into a creative oasis—one that he would inhabit and enjoy often, yet never want to live in. And besides, he had his own home. Despite this, it often felt like 'our' home, not just mine.

While I had the perfect home to write while we were together—and I did write a lot—I couldn't stretch my courage to turning my words into public works. As I've already shared, I'd lost my purpose to publish.

It's widely recommended that the first thing you must do after a romantic heartbreak is to remove all evidence of the person from your life. Many times after the end I considered emptying my home of anything that reminded me of him, which was almost everything from my largest, most exquisite painting to my bedside table and lamp. There was almost nothing in my home that he didn't bring to it.

> **It's a statement of commitment to yourself, to your healing and to your writing**

Yet it was me that asked for it. I see clearly now that in doing so, I was hoping he'd want in on it. Realising (and releasing) this now, is quite cathartic.

Looking around today, I feel no remorse at how my once empty apartment became my creative nest. I see it as his gift to me, an expression of the love he was capable of and an act of kindness. I have no desire to remove or destroy a thing, just to add to its beauty with my own finds from vintage shops and nature. I am at peace with it.

Not a day goes by that I do not recognise the incredible privilege I have to be able to live, love and create here. Thanks to this space, and thanks to my heartbreak, I can now fully return to my promise to not only write but publish.

Designing your own creative nest is a fabulously joyful exercise. And it doesn't require a huge budget, just an imaginative and inventive eye. It's a statement of commitment to yourself, to your healing and to your writing. And it's a strong statement to the other inhabitants of your home that you're serious about your craft and to leave you in peace with it.

A room of your own. A desk of your own. A corner of your own. Whatever you need, create it. You'll look neither backwards nor forwards but only at the glorious moments right in front of you, untethered and uninterrupted in your own sweet writer's hidey-hole. And the best thing? Your writing will reward you for it. Always.

Reflection and Action
Create a vision for your writing room,
space or desk then go and build it.

6. The Moment
On Knowing

We were born with our art in our heart. To paint, sing, draw, act, dance, design, make, play and express ourselves was our birthright and our human-right. We were destined to be creative beings not merely human doings.

Then along came school and our wild, curious, expressive essence began to die.

We learnt that numeracy and literacy were more valuable than play and creativity. We were indoctrinated to revere numbers and letters over sound and colour. We were told that a creative life would not pay the bills, that we should pursue something more sensible—and profitable.

If we did choose to exercise our creative licence, often at a most vulnerable moment in our lives, some other human, with no justification, took a sledgehammer to it. A well-meaning teacher, parent or friend said something that made us believe we had no talent. The sledgehammer may have delivered one swift blow that killed it off once and for all. Or it might have been a series of tiny taps over the years denting our creative confidence until it retreated and died.

We had a teacher tell us we'd never become a singer that day we sang one note off-key. We had parents directing us away from acting towards a more high-brow, well-paying profession. We put down our writing pens the day our careers adviser told us we had a talent for numbers and a future in accounting. We allowed others to become the judge and jury of our artistic merits, even though they had no right to sit on the bench.

And so it is with writers. We were born to turn our imagination into words, to tell our stories, to write with a wild heart about our passions. However, as we progressed through school, we weren't encouraged to write unbridled. Instead, we wrote to the rules and regulations of the education system. It judged us on our ability to comprehend prescribed texts mostly of no real interest to us. Then we were forced to produce essays on that text and endure standardised tests that graded and ranked us against our peers.

If writing was our purpose, we never really knew it. Is it any wonder the world is filled with lost and languishing, yet brilliant, writers?

I was an average English student in my final year of high school, first because I had no real enthusiasm for the curriculum texts. Second, because my English teacher had no real enthusiasm for me, or in seeing me succeed. As a result, I ended my school years with no idea I had a deep fascination for the written word. No idea that words could be my salvation. No inkling that I might've been born for it.

No doubt you have this book in your hands because there have been moments, maybe one very special stand-out moment, where you suspected writing might be your calling. You'll know it was *the* moment because you'll recall exactly where and when and how you created a piece of work, often years after the fact. You'll recall the minutest details of it all and how you felt. Happy. Focused. In flow.

'Writing is the only thing that when I do it, I don't feel I should be doing something else,' said one of my favourite writers, feminists and activists, Gloria Steinem. This is what you're looking for, that experience where you knew that writing might just be it.

My own moment occurred in 2006 at aged forty-two, twenty-four years after high school.

It crept up on me after a couple of years of writing newsletters for my own marketing business and clients—mostly sales material promoting the benefits of some product or service. I realised one day that while I loved the act of writing, the content itself was boring.

> **We were born to turn our imagination into words, to tell our stories, to write with a wild heart about our passions.**

I wondered what might happen if I were to direct my words towards something more creatively fulfilling. It's widely known that most professional copywriters, advertisers and marketers are frustrated artists or writers. I was one.

So, I decided to attempt to write my first book. I'd been teaching marketing to small business owners for a while, so a marketing book seemed like the perfect addition to my work. It would make marketing fun, practical and do-able for small-business people with little know-how, time or money.

As a single mum with an eight-year-old and a growing business, I was uncertain how I would create the space and time to write the book. Impatient woman that I am, it was untenable to write just a few words each day and let it unfold indefinitely. I had to do something grander to bring the book to life.

My own private writer's retreat was the answer. I took the next opportunity when Billy was with his father to take five days away from my home-office and clients. I was offered free-of-charge the use of a tiny, secluded cabin in the bush a two-hour drive south of Sydney.

> **Think of writing as your new and impassioned lover. Give yourself a chance to romance it, to fall hopelessly into the chasm of new love.**

If you have the courage and the means, you should undertake grand gestures for your writing too. Take a stretch of time to devote yourself to it. Find a fresh place to create. Try house-swaps or house-sitting if you're strapped for cash. Think of writing as your new and impassioned lover. Give yourself a chance to romance it, to fall hopelessly into the chasm of new love.

The exact moment I arrived at the cabin remains a vivid memory. As I pulled up, the owner stood there in an oversized overcoat to greet me. She was a plump, warm woman with a wide, generous smile. Stepping out of the car, the temperature felt like all of two degrees Celsius. What was I thinking? I was there to write with a fury but I wondered if my fingers would succumb to frostbite and refuse to do their work.

After showing me around, the owner left and I unpacked the car. I had all the essentials: nourishing pre-cooked meals, a woolly jumper, Ugg boots, my yoga mat, music, herbal teas and, of course, my laptop.

The cabin was all of ten paces square with a tiny kitchenette, bathroom, an indoor toilet (thank God), a rickety old wooden kitchen table, four mismatched dining chairs and a comfortable, cosy double bed. It had a pot-bellied stove with red gum stacked to the ceiling and an oil heater for back up if the fire died.

The cherry on the cake, however, was the front porch and the jetty that extended into the centre of a tiny lake filled with long, willowy reeds. After unpacking and lighting the fire, I rugged up and strolled out on that jetty, taking in deep gulps of crisp country air and marvelling at the stars winking at me from the jet-black sky. In an instant, the frogs croaking in the murky water below became my new-found friends. They were serenading me, willing me to step into my creative prowess.

Are you with me? Are you right beside me looking up at that luminous night sky? As a writer, you must discover how to take your readers with you. You must imagine them there beside you, as invested in your story as you are. You want them to be your sidekicks, participants in your story, to take the journey alongside you.

For three months, I'd planned this book. I'd named it, developed the structure and interviewed the people for it. Now I had four nights and five days to see if I could turn it into a book. I'd even detoxed myself of all stimulants—alcohol, coffee, sugar—so I'd have a clear mind for writing clever words.

'It takes as much energy to wish as it does to plan,' said Eleanor Roosevelt. What was *my* plan? I had no idea how many words I could write, never having written a book before. So the plan became simply to commit to writing for twelve hours per day.

> You'll know the moment when you realised you were born to write, as a child or an adult. You may not have recognised it at the time, but I urge you to search for it.

I'd take five-minute breaks every hour to stroll onto the jetty and fill my lungs with fresh air. I'd begin every morning with yoga and I'd stroll around the lake for thirty minutes at midday. I'd have no contact with the outside world and sleep (or at least try) for eight hours each night. That was it.

At the end of the five days, I'd see what I had. In my mind, I'd either be a writer or a failure.

I realise now that was a harsh and unhelpful attitude. It's akin to committing yourself for life to a brand-new lover or ending the affair after only five days together. I want you to be kinder to yourself. You must trust your own nature and your writing, that if you are meant for each other, it will be so.

To save you a blow-by-blow account of every moment of these five days, I'll cut to the chase. On the final evening at nine o'clock I wrote my final word, saved the manuscript on my laptop and made a copy of it onto a compact disc. (There was no Dropbox or iCloud in those days.)

My creative isolation was finally, and sadly, over. I stood up from that rickety kitchen table, strode out to the end of that jetty and hollered: 'This. Is. It. This is what I want to do for the rest of my life.' I shared my joy with the ink-black sky above and the clamorous frogs below.

In fifty hours, I'd written thirty thousand words. Of course, the words were far from perfect, but my job was not to critique the work right there and then, it was merely to do the work, to get the words onto the page. I could worry about the quality later in the second and third edits.

Less than six months later, with the generous support of friends and business colleagues, *Small Business Big Brand* was published and launched in Sydney at Centennial Parklands restaurant with an audience of one hundred or more friends and clients.

Today, all these years later, I often take one of the last few remaining copies of the book from my bookshelf and tenderly flick through it. I notice all its imperfections. It feels sweet, earnest, innocent—and amateurish. But I'm grateful I found the courage to write it. It was my very first step to pursuing a writer's life.

You'll know the moment when you realised you were born to write, as a child or an adult. You may not have recognised it at the time but I urge you to search for it. Find it, dig into it, paint a picture of it in words. Etch it into your heart and brain. Use it as an anchor, a constant reminder of why you write.

Romantic love is much like writing. You know if it's meant for you. You just know. There's no second-guessing, no agonising, no anxiety. You feel happy and in flow. That doesn't mean it's easy, it just feels instinctively right. It's possible that a couple of those half-baked manuscripts would have been published by now if I'd listened to my instincts regarding my relationship early on. But then you would likely not be reading this book now. No use wondering but always trust your gut.

Reflection and Action
Write a story about the moment you knew
you were meant to write.

7. Your Story Matters
On Story-telling

You might think you've led a dead-boring life and that no one would want to read your story. Let me tell you right now. You are dead wrong—particularly if you are a woman.

I unapologetically address women here because I am one and can only write from my own experience, albeit as a privileged, middle-class, white woman. I do not wish to alienate you if you are a man. I ask you to support my plea to all women. Think of the women you love. Put yourself in their shoes awhile. Read this through their eyes. Then share this book with them.

So many women think our stories don't matter, so we ignore and suppress them instead of expressing and celebrating them.

The truth is, we need women's stories more than ever.

Women are sagacious story-tellers. Our stories reveal our innate wisdom. They connect us and unite us. They offer a refuge in a volatile and uncertain world. They are the portal for healing our private and collective sorrow so we may find hope again and take positive action.

Through sharing and examining our story we can start to write a new, more balanced account of our world. It's never been more vital because we simply can't allow his-story to continue to dominate our past and drive the future.

We can no longer suppress the stories of women. Just as we can't suppress the stories of our Indigenous people, LGBTQI people, people with disabilities and every other minority that doesn't fit within the dominant heteronormative white male culture of our times.

We'll struggle to close the gender gap within a system men have built for men. It reminds me of the American writer, feminist and civil rights activist, Audre Lorde's declaration, 'For the master's tools will never dismantle the master's house. They may allow us to temporarily beat him at his game, but they will never allow us to bring about genuine change'.

There's no doubt now that the unravelling of the man-made system is accelerating thanks to many brilliant women leading the way: Grace Tame, Jacinda Ardern, Esther Perel, Greta Thunberg and Malala Yousafzi are a few among many. In Australia, after the 2022 Federal election, we see unprecedented numbers of women leading change in our country from the Teal independent Monique Ryan to our first Aboriginal female Greens senator, Lidia Thorpe.

> Our stories reveal our innate wisdom. They connect us and unite us. They offer a refuge in a volatile and uncertain world. They are the portal for healing our private and collective sorrow so we may find hope again and take positive action.

Now is the perfect time for women to hasten change for a more just and equitable world. For the first time in my life, it feels possible. Change just might be happening faster than we ever conceived possible. If we can respond globally with such speed and force to a pandemic, surely we can respond with the same urgency to the emergency of gender inequality.

But how do ordinary women like you and I make a contribution? We don't have the name, the fame or the stage that these more public women possess.

Yet we do, because the state of our world starts with us. It starts right where we are now in our own homes, streets and communities. We can be the women whose stories spread like wildfire to other women, from home to home, from kitchen table to kitchen table and throughout our workplaces. For this is where real change begins.

To do this we must start with our own private stories. We must explore and examine our stories to understand how and why we're stuck and why we've obediently remained within the master's house. It's from here that we can write a new story, not just for women but for all of humanity and Mother Earth, and for the majority of men too—for many no longer wish to live within the master's house either.

Whether you agree with me or not is not my business. A writer shouldn't hide her political views, her staunch feminist values and her quest to disrupt the status quo. If she does, she risks being bland and boring. In the painful pursuit of trying to be everything to everybody—to please every reader—she'll end up being nobody to anybody. And her words will die an unnatural death long before their time.

To be a writer you need an opinion, an idea or a vision of the world you want to live in and the world you wish for your children and their children. You must share your stories of the past because in some way, big or small, you want to change the future. You must find the courage to tell them because they are the pathway to healing your grief, to creating something better for you and those around you.

Your stories truly do matter. And you do not have to be famous to tell them. A good ninety-five per cent of the world's women have lived extraordinarily ordinary lives. But every one of those women, including you, has a story to tell.

So where to start?

Photos are the perfect way. They are the most exquisite portal to your memories and your stories. They are always revelatory and they lead to new insights about yourself and your beliefs about the world.

Recently I found a photo of me standing with my three siblings outside the front of St Paul's Anglican Church in Naracoorte in rural South Australia. It was Sunday 26 September 1976 and I was twelve years old. I'm wearing a red polo-neck jumper under a respectable knee-length denim tunic, heavy-duty grey stockings and bright red platform shoes. There's a scowl on my face as I urge Mum to snap the photo so we can hightail it home.

I'd just rather reluctantly knelt at the church altar for the first time alongside other young people of our parish. We'd eaten the body and drunk the blood of Christ at our confirmation ceremony.

My confirmation was just one of the many memories of growing up with religion in my childhood. As a family, we attended church because that's what good law-abiding citizens did in those days. Every Sunday we'd dutifully turn up to the morning service and Sunday School to be taught that God's way was the right way—and the only way. I don't ever recall questioning if there was any other way.

We can be the women whose stories spread like wildfire to other women, from home to home, from kitchen table to kitchen table and throughout our workplaces.

Four years after that photo, at the age of sixteen, my parents gave me the choice to opt out of going to church. That was the year I lost my religion.

Sadly, however, I didn't lose the lesson from the story of Adam and Eve.

According to the Bible, Adam and Eve were the first two humans God created in the Garden of Eden. God formed the first human, Adam (the man), out of the dust of the earth. He then breathed life into Adam and made him the caretaker of the world.

'You've been created in my likeness and you have powers over everything you see. You are the master of it all,' God said. 'But do not eat the apples from the Tree of Knowledge or you will be banished and die.'

As much as Adam loved the animals and the garden, he soon became lonely.

So God created the second human, Eve (the wo-man), from the rib of Adam so she could become his loyal and obedient wife and servant. Some biblical scholars claim that Eve may have been made from Adam's penis. Seriously?

One day, a sinister serpent convinced Eve to pluck an apple from the tree. Eve took a bite of the forbidden fruit then enticed Adam to take a bite too. In devouring the delicious apple, they committed what subsequent generations of Christians came to know as the original sin— the sin of disobedience. Soon a mighty voice filled the air from above. 'You are banished to live life on Earth to fend for yourself until you die,' boomed God.

So here we have a myth that tells us wo-man was made of man, that Adam in a sense gave birth to Eve. Is this not the ultimate insult to women? Not only that, but Adam was also Eve's master and ruler, always her superior. And finally, Eve was the temptress, the initiator of the original sin. It was her fault they were banished from the Garden of Eden.

This is why, more than ever, we need every woman's version of the past, our side of the story.

I'm sorry if you're a true believer and this story troubles your Christian traditions. As I've said, a writer must have an opinion, a belief to share lest her work falls like that tree in the forest that nobody hears. It will not be to everyone's liking. If you're considering abandoning this book, perhaps you might read on and find the will to write the counter-argument instead?

> **You must share your stories of the past because in some way, big or small, you want to change the future.**

The Bible is the most read book in the world. It's no wonder millions of women are still living their lives in the image of Eve.

But there's another take on the Adam and Eve story, one that's not so well-known and doesn't appear in the Bible. It's controversial and debated hotly among feminists, academics and Jewish scholars.

According to Jewish folklore, Adam's first wife wasn't Eve. She was Lilith.

The story goes that Lilith was born of the same soil as Adam and she shared the Garden of Eden with him before Eve. Problems arose when Adam tried to exercise dominance over Lilith during intercourse. She believed they were created equal so she should not have to lay beneath him or submit to his commands.

Forced to choose between submitting to her husband or leaving the Garden of Eden, Lilith chose exile. Soon afterwards, God sent three angels to retrieve her but she refused to return with them and turned her back on God, preferring a life of independence. Lilith was demonised for her decision to reject the Creator and was now widely considered as the 'woman-shaped demon' and accused of inflicting death upon thousands of new-born babies.

> **Before you know it, you're writing down a rabbit hole. The story is leading you. You're no longer in the driver's seat.**

Without his wife, Adam became lonely and so God made him a new wife, Eve. Later, Lilith was said to be jealous of Adam and Eve so she disguised herself as the serpent and tricked Eve into picking and eating the forbidden fruit.

Stories abound about Lilith. While Christian texts portray her as evil for her disobedience and rejection of Adam and God, in many other ancient cultures she is seen as a Goddess and a symbol for the liberation of women. She stands for sexual empowerment, wisdom, knowledge, independence and the right for women to think for themselves and not conform to the dominant patriarchal culture.

While Lilith was condemned for her rejection of this culture, Eve was admired for her subservience and held up as a role-model for all women to follow to this day.

I wonder how our world would have evolved if Adam and Lilith had embraced equality. What if they'd been able to reach an agreement on equality? Or what if Eve had been made first and given birth to Adam, as women actually do?

So many myths. So many questions. So many possibilities.

I wish I'd learned the legend of Lilith instead of Eve as a young girl. I might have made some radically different decisions as I became a woman, particularly in my romantic choices. I can see clearly that my inner-Eve was at play at times in my last relationship, even all these years later.

That feels gut-wrenching to admit.

See where your story can take you? You select a photo and recall what was going on in that moment of your life. You compare your beliefs then to your beliefs now and notice the gaping difference. You ponder on why and how you changed. You start thinking about the experiences of your life that disproved the story society has indoctrinated you to believe. And an idea springs to mind.

Before you know it, you're writing down a rabbit hole. The story is leading you. You're no longer in the driver's seat. Your words are in control, not you. The story wants to be written through you. And then you type The End. You may even cry.

Scan your life and collect your stories. Some will be joyful. Others painful. All will be invaluable. There is a lesson in every story. Some of them you learned at the time. Others you may only understand years later as you write them.

Then share your stories, no matter how long or short or good or bad you believe you are at shaping them into words. Then try speaking to them. Write then tell. Or tell then write.

I don't care which way you do it. Just find a way. Any way—because your story matters.

Reflection and Action

Find a photo that reveals a defining moment of your life.
Write the story.

8. Interested and Interesting
On Story-catching

Stories are the greatest way to make sense of, and heal from, grief. When we tell them at just the right time to just the right person, they can change and even save that person's life. That alone is the reason to dig them up and share them with others.

After divulging my misery at the end of love to my friend, Stephen Whitteridge, he didn't give me unsolicited advice, throw me a pity-party or interrogate me for the gut-wrenching details. He simply told me a story.

For fourteen years he'd volunteered at a hostel in Sydney—a well-known shelter and support service provider for homeless men. His job was to serve the men breakfast while offering a compassionate ear listening to their stories. The manager of the shelter had been working in a full-time paid capacity for many years. One day, he shared with Stephen that he was being made redundant and that he was very anxious about his future.

The cleaner at the hostel, a quiet, elderly man, was sweeping the floor nearby, focused intently on his work and not a part of the conversation. 'He had not uttered one word in all the years I'd known him,' Stephen said. 'Then all of a sudden, he shuffled up to us, looked the manager in the eye with kindness and said, "empty hand catch new ball" and then he just shuffled back to work.'

This simple touching story made me laugh out loud. I was startled by the sense of freedom it engendered as I suddenly wondered what new ball might appear on the horizon. It left me feeling calm, curious and hopeful again. It turns out that it was not a new lover but this book.

Stories are everywhere. They appear in conversations. They come through observations. They emerge from asking thoughtful questions. 'It is obvious that the only interesting people are interested people, and to be completely interested is to have forgotten about *I*,' said Alan Watts, the famous English philosopher, teacher and Zen master. The most wondrous story-tellers are curiously interested people who forget about themselves.

To be a brilliant story-teller, you must become a story-catcher. Put up your anecdote antenna every time you walk out the door. Keep your mind inquisitive and your eyes and ears open. Ask yourself regularly, 'is there a story in this? If so, what is its point? How could I use it?' Then find a way to catch it quickly. Keep a notebook in your handbag, a word document always open on your laptop, a notes file on your phone or use voice memos or take a photo or video. Before you know it, you'll have a library full of potential stories.

While it's easy to look outside ourselves to stories like Stephen's, it's much harder to look inside at our private past life stories. Yet the most meaningful stories are always from within. While this might seem contradictory to Alan Watt's advice to forget about *I,* your own stories are the invisible thread to connect you to another human. They turn that *I* into *us*.

If you're wondering how this is relevant to fictional story-telling, every piece of fiction was once a kernel of that author's own story. You may not know it as a reader but I promise the story sprang from the depths of that person's real life. That's why your own story is the most powerful place to start. It's like the story of my confirmation which turned into the story of Lilith which might become the inspiration for a feminist novel. Watch this space.

The most wondrous story-tellers are curiously interested people who forget about themselves.

Where do you even start to capture the stories of your private life? Here are a couple of ideas. They continue to work for me; maybe they'll work for you too.

The first is an idea I've called *Story-boxing*. Lockdown gave me the perfect opportunity to dig up and reflect on my life stories. One day I dragged out my many boxes filled with the precious memorabilia I'd collected over my life: cards, letters, trinkets, school reports, childhood books (and Bibles), journals, certificates but mostly photos. I found a smaller, plain white box and wrote on the outside of it 'Me & My Life'.

For a couple of days, I sorted through every box and reflected on each item and photo. Then I filled the small box with the special photos and items that marked the most significant experiences and events of my life. It brought up all sorts of emotions, both painful and joyful. It was this activity, by the way, that uncovered that 1976 photo from my confirmation.

Two significant thoughts occurred to me during this process. The first was that I was far more winsome than I ever thought I was as I grew up. Vain? No. There's not a woman alive who doesn't need to remind herself that she was once a gorgeous girl. It was distressing to think I'd wasted so much time, money and energy trying to make myself more beautiful than I naturally was. Even that little insight could lead to a story, perhaps even a chapter of that feminist novel.

> **Your own stories are the invisible thread to connect you to another human. They turn that *I* into us.**

The second was that I'd had many more happy life experiences than sad ones. I recognised that I'd often felt trapped in the painful experiences while not really acknowledging or appreciating all the joyful ones. One of the greatest human afflictions is our bias towards negativity, that we most strongly attach to the hurtful moments and bereavements rather than the good times and our achievements.

Despite this, I continue to believe our most painful and grievous experiences are those from which we learn the most. Despair is our greatest teacher. Grief is what makes us kinder humans. It could be private heartbreak over lost love or sorrow at the devastating destruction of our natural world (and humans). Pain processed through story will always lead us to our purpose. It turns our apathy into activism for a cause greater than ourselves. Like my confirmation story again. While it began with *me*, it became a story about *we*, one to hopefully inspire all women towards liberation.

The second way to capture your life stories is through *Story-timelining*, another process I began during lockdown. I first heard about the concept from my writers' group friend, Yamini Naidu.

Here's how it works. Create a simple table with four columns in a Word document. In the first column entitled *Year*, record every year from your birthdate till now. In the second column entitled *Events and Places*, record the facts, places and major events of each year as far as you can remember; where you were living (having lived in ten towns and twenty-six houses this was quite a feat for me); where you went to school; significant occasions or events like births, deaths, marriages, divorces, family celebrations, jobs or businesses you owned; or works you've created; travel and holidays and so on.

And now to the most interesting yet challenging third column entitled *What happened?* Using memorabilia or a photo from that year, if you have one, jog your memory and jot down notes. What took place? Where were you? Who was there? What were you thinking and feeling? Why was this experience so important? How did it influence your future? What are you still holding onto, if anything? What do you need to let go of, if anything? What would you tell your seven-year-old self now? Your fourteen-year-old self? Your twenty-one-year-old self? And so on. These are random notes with no real rhyme or reason.

Now to that fourth column titled *Story Idea*. Ask yourself, is there a story here? Is there something that would be healing for you to write? Is there a lesson or piece of wisdom you're being called to impart? Would a potential reader find this interesting and helpful? If so, write a short sentence with a single compelling idea. Whether that idea will become a story of fact or fiction is not your business just yet. Your job is just to get your notes down so one day you can get to work on your story.

> **Pain processed through story will always lead us to our purpose. It turns our apathy into activism for a cause greater than ourselves.**

My own timeline document is a very messy array of incomplete notes and ideas. It will be a work-in-progress till the day I die, no doubt. Interestingly, this process revealed a pattern in my love-life and the numerous relationships I've had over the past twenty years. Overall, it divulged a history of choosing unavailable men and it made me consider that I had perhaps chosen these men because I was in some way unavailable too. With the first twenty years of my adult life in a traditional monogamous relationship, perhaps the next twenty years were meant to be a bit messy and experimental on the love front.

I've ruminated a lot recently over the dominant societal story that having a partner is necessary for a complete and happy life. I've witnessed increasing numbers of women of my age opening themselves up to a more expansive love rather than an exclusive one—for other women, for their community and for Mother Nature.

Maybe it's not my karma to find 'the one' and grow old with them in this lifetime. And maybe it is. Anything is possible. As I recover from this heartbreak and put myself out there again, I will trust that if there is one special person meant for me, they won't pass me by.

See what timelining your life—and loves—might reveal to you? If you choose to do this, don't let it daunt you. I suggest you just get started. Do it in one year or seven-year increments if that works for you. Do one hour a week on it. Make it a fun activity with your parents, siblings, partner, kids or childhood friends. Maybe everyone can complete their own timeline and you can cross-check your memory of events at a celebration meal together? Make a game of it.

Does this sound too much for you? You're not so organised or interested in devoting yourself to this activity? Don't worry. Try the lucky-dip approach instead. Take that huge box of old photos out of the garage, close your eyes, stick your hand in and pull-out photo after photo until you find one that piques your curiosity and gets your fingers itching to write. Or scroll back through your digital photo library and choose one that has a back story.

Or just think back to when you were seven, fourteen, twenty-one, twenty-eight, thirty-five and so on. What was happening in your life then? Perhaps a significant event calls you to breathe life into it in words. And, of course, there's the grief that brought you to this book too. Put them all in your timeline and dig into them.

As soon as you see the emergence of a single story that might heal and that lights you up inside, start writing and don't stop. That single story might turn into a whole book. And that single book might become a series of books. Or it might just turn into your first blog, a piece to submit to a newspaper, an online media publication or that story competition you just found through an online search. Who knows?

One final thought, the flipside of my somewhat earnest invitation to you. I want you to be curious rather than serious about this story-telling business. I want you to have some fun with it, to catch your stories with amusement and wonder and treat them like that child threading beads.

Reflection and Action
How will you capture your stories?
Start the story-boxing or story-timelining exercise.

9. Letting Go
On Story-releasing

Sunday is my day of rest. You'll need a regular reprieve from writing too, lest you become obsessive. Just as you need a break from your family or work, you'll need a break from your words. Take time off to celebrate your achievements, to replenish yourself and reconnect with the world outside so you can create anew with fresh eyes.

I guarantee, however, that your words won't leave your heart or mind while you're off-duty. That was me one day as I was out on a bush-walk attempting to immerse myself in an audio book by Stephen Jenkinson called *Come of Age*. It's a profound book on elderhood. I recommend it if you're committed to living the last quarter of your life in service to others. Yet I caught myself regularly tuning out from his dulcet tones and deliberating over the next bead I'd thread on this necklace of a book.

Thanks to Stephen's inspiration, by the time I'd walked in the door I was certain of the next morning's story. Happily, I laid my mind to rest and went about creating a sumptuous, healthy dinner for myself. Self-nourishment and self-care are essential foundations for reaching your creative heights. They directly contradict the puerile, out-dated narrative that artists must be starving, penniless, substance-addicted crazies for their brilliance to emerge.

The next morning as I awoke and began journaling about the story, I became uncertain. I was second-guessing myself. It didn't feel like the right story to write that day. This will happen to you too. One moment you'll be certain of your next step, then conviction will desert you. That's the writer's lot in life. All I can advise is to listen to it. Follow it. Allow your uncertainty to take you where it must. Don't put a lid on it or you'll be left wondering 'what if?' It may bring you back to where you began or it may lead you to something greater than you'd ever believed possible.

Something bothered me from yesterday's story. It came to me in a flash. A sense of guilt prevailed. I wondered if I'd done you a great disservice, my dear reader. I'd just dumped this monumental task on you to dig up the stories of your past without warning you of the potential fall-out. I hadn't warned you that examining your past life stories would bring up buried, painful emotions or re-open old wounds that could have harmful side-effects.

> **The purpose of examining your stories is to release yourself from them.**

I hadn't warned you this experience would be like self-administered therapy, that in a way, it's comparable to undergoing psychological treatment. If you find yourself struggling as you explore, I urge you to seek support. Support might come from a wise friend, a professional therapist, a twelve-step group, a doctor or family member who has your back—and, of course, your own writers' group. Whatever you need, seek help and you will find it. Do not suffer alone.

And here's the most poignant point of the whole book.

The purpose of examining your stories is to release yourself from them.

In Zen, Ensō is a circle drawn in one or two uninhibited brushstrokes to express a moment when the mind is free to let the body create. It expresses the reality that everything that has a beginning has its time and its end. It signifies absolute enlightenment, strength, elegance, the universe and mu (the void).

Some Ensō symbols are closed loops, while others are left open. I'm particularly drawn to the open loop and the void at the end of the brushstroke. In this space the words of Viktor Frankl, the famed Holocaust survivor, world-renowned psychiatrist and author of *Man's Search for Meaning*, seem most fitting. 'Between stimulus and response there is a space. In that space is our power to choose our response. In our response lies our growth and our freedom.'

Some endings, such as the closing of the seasons, occur gradually without us really noticing. Other endings, such as the sudden death of a loved one or the loss of a job are abrupt and traumatic and turn our life upside down in an instant. Yet other endings, such as the end of a marriage, occur slowly, often agonisingly over time.

Absolutely everything that begins has an end. Some endings we choose. Many we don't. Endings can be delightful or distressing. They can offer relief or send us into despair. Nothing will stop an ending if it is meant to be. Endings occur because something new is waiting to emerge.

Rage and sorrow savaged me at the end of my relationship. I couldn't do much at all for two weeks. Still, it was a weirdly serene space at times, like the mu, a gap in which to fully release the man and the hope I'd bestowed upon our relationship. It was in this space of surrender that the idea for this book emerged and where I chose to release the old story so I could write a new one.

And this is how we must treat the stories of our life—as a series of beginnings and endings. By examining our stories, we might notice a tiny crack or a huge chasm (the void) at the end of the story where we had an opportunity to respond differently and choose freedom and growth. We have a choice to liberate ourselves from our stories or remain stuck in them. Most of us, including me more often than I dare admit, unconsciously choose the latter. We opt for staying stuck because it's what we know and it's more comfortable. In so doing, we repeat past patterns instead of breaking them.

You might think this only applies to the grievous or injurious experiences and heartbreaks of your life, the ones that left you battered and bewildered. You might believe you should forget the (perceived) negative and hang on to the (perceived) positive tales. Not so. I believe you must release them all—the great, the gruesome, the heart-breaking and the heart-healing.

That doesn't mean you let go of the memory. It doesn't mean you re-write them with an entirely new ending. Nor does it mean you lock them away never to be repeated. What it means is that you don't attach yourself to the stories. You don't make them your identity. You don't allow them to continue to direct your life.

While your stories might reveal how you got to where you are and offer fabulous fuel for your writing, they are not the essence of who you are. They are not a reliable signpost for your future. They are no indicator of your full potential or the arbiter of what's humanly possible for you. They're a grounding and intriguing place to start, but that's all.

Nothing will stop an ending if it is meant to be. Endings occur because something new is waiting to emerge.

In 2013, almost three years after returning from France, I was about to turn fifty and the manuscript for *Unstuck in Provence* lay dormant, untouched and unfinished, buried in my computer. I hadn't found the courage to publish such a private account of my heartbreak in my travel memoirs as yet. So, I took a month off work with the sole purpose to edit my book and overcome my fear. Just months later, we launched it at a fun French-themed soirée in Melbourne. Sharing the book with others was like a final release. No doubt it will be so with this one too.

'Owning our story can be hard but not nearly as difficult as spending our lives running from it. Embracing our vulnerabilities is risky but not nearly as dangerous as giving up on love and belonging and joy – the experiences that make us most vulnerable. Only when we are brave enough to explore the darkness will we discover the infinite power of our light,' said the well-known social researcher and story-teller on vulnerability, shame and empathy, Brené Brown.

So, own your story, do not run from it. Then please remember, you are not your story. Let it go so you can live and love anew.

Now let's forget about you and me awhile. Let's turn this same idea outwards and get some perspective. We must consider how our personal story is just a tiny piece of the collective story of our sisters around the world, our Indigenous people, our own family and ancestors and Mother Earth. And on it goes. While our stories are significant, they are but one tiny piece of a giant cosmic story puzzle, which is the reason why we must all share them.

By viewing our stories as insignificant in the scheme of the universe, we somehow find the courage to offer them to other women. While still important, they no longer have a hold on us. We let go of the fear of being judged, ridiculed and maybe even persecuted by voicing our truth. And we give permission to other women to write and share their stories too. Imagine a world of women gathering in our homes, writing and sharing our stories and threading bead after exquisite bead while fashioning a better future.

There's no doubt the human race is sitting in the void right now. We're in between stories, letting go of the old so we can create anew. We're at the beginning again. This is why women must let our stories go and get on with producing new stories. See why we must use our writing will and story-telling powers for a world beyond ourselves? There's never been a better time.

Reflection and Action
What story or stories do you need to write and release?

10. Freethinking Forebears
On Ancestral Elders

I contemplate death on occasions, not because I plan to exit this not-so-heavenly earth any time soon, but because by deliberating on my mortality, I might just be more compelled to live my best life. As Mark Twain said, 'The fear of death follows from the fear of life. A [human] who lives fully, is prepared to die at any time.'

It reminds me of that clichéd old exercise of writing your own eulogy. That said, it's not such a bad idea, particularly if you've been blocked or not yet begun your writing endeavours. Consider the stories you'd want shared about you by a loved one at your funeral and journal about them. It may just be the very task required to incite action and ignite your writing.

Thanks to the words of Stephen Jenkinson in his case for elderhood, I've become less worried about the end and more concerned about the years directly ahead. His words have given me the confidence to believe that my nearing sixty years of wisdom are worth sharing with those who seek them. He inspires me to defy our ageist society and advance the cause of eldership instead. I figure I have a good thirty years to live, all going well. It's exciting to consider the possibilities. Writing many more books is only a portion of the plan.

My maternal grandfather, my Papa, Gordon Alexander Coad, was a wise and wonderful elder. If I could host a Deep Dinner and invite anyone dead or alive, Stephen and Gordon would have prominent seats at the dining table together. (Deep Dinners are intimate dining events where people gather to share their story and explore deep themes such as purpose, death and climate-change—and, of course, grief and loss. Who would you invite to your Deep Dinner?)

During one of our COVID lockdowns I rediscovered an old photo album of my Papa's that had been entrusted to me as his oldest grandchild. On opening the front cover, a photo of him fell out at my feet. It was a close up of him sitting in his favourite armchair staring knowingly into the camera with warm eyes and a gentle smile. He was seventy years of age and gravely ill. He knew he didn't have long to live, yet there was no fear on his face and no tinge of regret.

It caused an eruption of tears. Regret that I didn't really know this kind-hearted man overcame me. I was thirty years old when he died too young, just a year after the photo was taken. We'd had plenty of time to become the best of companions. I don't know why we weren't. If only I'd valued him then as I've come to value him posthumously, maybe things could have been different. I long to re-write our history together.

Gordon was born a farmer's son in Nhill Victoria in 1921 and was raised on the family property in the Serviceton and Wolseley area. His parents were strict Church of Christ parishioners. No dancing. No booze. No fun. Three times every Sunday, Gordon attended church with his sisters. By all accounts, it was his narrow-minded upbringing as a child that later turned him into a broad-minded man.

Gordon's passions were planes, poetry, music, books, sport, amateur radio, exploring new ideas and inventions—not so much farming. He was also passionate about people and a real community-builder. Always interested. Always interesting. A freethinker. At eighteen, he was desperate to enlist and train as a pilot or radio operator in World War Two. However, his father and his country needed him on the land growing crops and fattening livestock for the war effort. A farmer's life was his lot.

As Mark Twain said, 'The fear of death follows from the fear of life. A [human] who lives fully, is prepared to die at any time.'

At the end of the war, he married my Nana, Elva May Wallis and had four children, the eldest being my mother, Joy. Their farmhouse was built about three long stone throws from his parents' home on the same property.

As I was growing up, once a year as a family we'd visit for a week's holiday filled with adventure. The farmhouse was an assemblage of rooms built of whatever building materials were available during the scarcity of wartime along with pine floorboards and a red tin roof. The place for family gatherings was a hearty kitchen dominated by a solid wood kitchen table just an arm's length from the old wood-fired stove.

A long-drop toilet could be found a good twenty metres out the back down a dirt path. The journey to the toilet would take us past Papa's radio room at the back of the house. In this room, he'd either be smoking rollies (self-rolled cigarettes) or chewing PK gum with his Ham (amateur) radio in hand. He'd peer out through the one small dusty window, one eye cocked to the weather, the other on the radio tower. He'd prattle on with men in country towns on the other side of Australia, fishermen off the coast of Indonesia (in what language remains a mystery) and his best mate on the neighbouring farm.

> **Consider the stories you'd want shared about you by a loved one at your funeral and journal about them.**

In this room Papa studied to become a pilot before obtaining his license in 1959. It was the room where he stored his electronic gadgets, his footy training kit, other sporting paraphernalia and various inventions. Later in life, it was home for his keyboard piano, his record player and a vast collection of vinyl records where he'd compose and play music long into the night. Alongside family and farming, this was his life.

The path to the toilet also led past Nana's laundry, a room that housed a cement washtub, a hand wringer and wicker laundry baskets filled with clothes to be pegged out on three lines that criss-crossed the bone-dry dirt yard. As a child, it was a scary trek to the toot by torchlight at night. I always wondered if I'd make it back alive or if I'd be found dead in the morning from a redback spider bite, underpants still around my ankles.

A tennis court flanked one side of the house. There were holes in the fences, weeds poking through the cracks in the asphalt and a droopy tennis net requiring constant winding up to the requisite height. Despite its forlorn state, it was where family tennis and cricket tournaments were won and lost and it was the birthplace for my mother's love of tennis, a game she still plays today.

On a hot day, Nana would relax on the front porch overlooking the buffalo-grass lawn and Peace rose bushes while we'd squirt each other with the hose, hopping around in a mad scramble to avoid bees. No holiday was complete without yabbying in the dam, spotlighting rabbits at night or watching the shearers shear sheep after sheep.

Farming was a lonely life and Gordon was a real people-person. Legend has it that he'd regularly take the tractor into town for repairs in the morning and not return home until dinner. He'd while away the day chatting with the townsfolk. It was much preferred to a day alone ploughing the paddocks. While Papa was a great talker and a committed practical joker, he was also a curiously deep thinker and a thoughtful listener.

In 1970, Gordon's beloved wife Elva died of breast cancer at the age of fifty. Two years later he married Bev, a woman with four young children. Just when his first four children had all begun to leave home, he became an instant father again.

> **Now every time I write, a little piece of Papa pours out of me onto the page.**

Ten years later at the age of fifty-nine, Gordon and Bev retired from the farm and moved into Bordertown. It was here that his true passions—radio, communications, music and community—would finally merge into one. Everything he'd loved over the years finally came together in one grand idea—5TCBFM radio station—the first community radio station of its kind in South Australia. The first transmission went to air from his lounge room in 1981. Gordon was a happy, happy man. He'd finally brought his creative dreams to life.

Now, some forty years later, Gordon's legacy lives on. The community radio station has a small staff and many volunteers. One of his greatest legacies was his mentorship of young people, teaching them about music and how to become great communicators of the air.

In 1989, his emphysema finally forced him to retire from his beloved radio station. Four years later, I was living and working in Port Moresby, Papua New Guinea, when the awful call came. It was from my mother telling me Papa did not have long to live. I'm so glad I made the lightning trip home to see him before he died just weeks later.

Through writing Papa's story, I feel closer to him. He's become my ancestral elder, my creative muse and silent adviser. When I doubt my work or when a wave of grief hits, I look at this photo and ask him for guidance. His response is always compassionate yet firm. His inner footy trainer comes out. 'Stop worrying, keep writing,' he says, 'and keep your eyes on the ball.'

Papa's story was also the motivation for a recent road-trip with my mother back to my birthplace, the farm and the radio station. It was a nostalgic and heart-warming excursion yet one that raised many questions I didn't know how to ask, mostly about the history of the Aboriginal people who first lived on Papa's land. One day, when I find the courage (and the time), I'll go investigating and perhaps write a book. So many books to write, so little time. Sigh.

Now every time I write, a little piece of Papa pours out of me onto the page.

You are the sum of your thousands of ancestors. Every time you write, a little part of them pours out of you too. I hope among those thousands, you have at least one wise ancestral elder you might call on, alive or dead. An elder to turn to when you're baffled and beaten, when you think your writing stinks or when you feel like doing anything but confronting the blank page or the keyboard.

Go and find that freethinking forebear, the one who went left when all your other ancestors seemed to turn right, to conform. Find the one who was true to themselves. The one who pursued their creative passions: the writer, the painter, the musician, the one who made living creatively their way of life. Investigate them. Get to know them. Learn to love them and see where it leads you. And, of course, write their story.

Reflection and Action

Who is your ancestral elder?
Find a photo and write their story.

11. Who's Your Heroine?
On Writing Icons

Elizabeth Gilbert is my writing shero. She's the next person I'd invite to that imaginary Deep Dinner. Do you have a literary hero or heroine—a genius whose words inspire you to write? If not, I recommend you choose one. They're the perfect companion to your ancestral elder but they play a different role in your writing.

Your ancestral elder offers wise counsel. They lived (or still live) a creative life. While their artistic endeavours may have taken a completely different turn to yours, they're your stimulus to keep writing. They're a comforting, familial anchor to turn to in order to write through your grief. They can will you to do the work when you can't find the will in yourself.

A hero or heroine on the other hand is a writer like you. They've written for aeons, possibly many moons before you ever got started. You adore their work and they've excelled at it. They've experimented and succeeded and failed in the pursuit of becoming a better, bolder, braver writer. They've made writing their life's work.

They may or may not have gained notoriety, sold millions of books or made the big bucks. That's not important. They are brilliant (according to you, anyway) at what they do and you revere their work. They motivate you to pursue excellence in your own writing.

Your writing icon should not be someone you want to emulate. That's not the point of a hero or heroine. Do not aim to become them. And do not compare your work to theirs—comparison is a hapless exercise.

It's the thief of creative joy and the surest path to self-doubt and self-destruction.

The point of an icon is that their work lights you up and inspires you to write from your wildest, most courageous heart. They're someone who has done the hard work to succeed and who is vulnerable in sharing the perils of their writer's life. They're someone whose work you can study and learn from.

In 2008, I took off to the United States with a dozen copies of *Small Business Big Brand* packed in bubble-wrap at the bottom of my luggage. I had a garage-full to try and sell so I thought I'd try to crack the largest market in the world—America.

I decided to take a three-week trip, the first two weeks for business and the last for a much-needed holiday. Before leaving, I'd arranged meetings with people in the publishing and PR industries and booked myself to deliver a couple of talks and attend a few events.

'It was my delusion and naivety that brought me here,' Lady Gaga once said. That was me to a tee, deluded and naïve in equal measures. Sadly, my delusion and naivety didn't bring me the fame and fortune of Lady Gaga.

> **The point of an icon is that their work lights you up and inspires you to write from your wildest, most courageous heart.**

Here I was thinking I'd penetrate the world's premier sales frontier with a few paltry meetings in two weeks and return home a raving success. However, it was my first step towards putting my words out to the world beyond the comfort of my hometown. And who knew what might come of it?

On the third week of my US sojourn, at the last minute, I decided to end my trip with a novel holiday experience. With very limited funds and little interest in sight-seeing alone in Los Angeles, I booked myself into a low-cost, six-day health retreat at Desert Hot Springs, a three-hour drive from Los Angeles airport.

In the airport bookshop as I was awaiting my car transfer, I stumbled upon *Eat Pray Love,* the book that shot Gilbert to stardom. It seemed like the perfect company for a week of fasting and detoxing in isolation.

Looking back now, that whole US trip was made memorable and enjoyable because of this book. It provided the comfort I needed as I licked my wounds at the lack of book sales success. But mostly it inspired me to keep writing with heart and courage. It gave me permission to write more authentically and vulnerably about my own life and beliefs.

That same copy of EPL still sits in my bookshelf all these years later. The pages are crinkly, withered and dog-eared thanks to the hot-water springs and the sauna where I'd devoured every word.

Yet there is no doubt *Eat Pray Love* has divided women across the world. I've just as many friends that loathed it as loved it. This should give you comfort though and remind you not to write to appeal to everyone. You must write to appeal to yourself first and trust others will love your words too.

You must believe that one day you'll inspire someone else to make you their writing icon. Is that not another universal purpose for your writing—to inspire other women to roll up their sleeves and write too?

Following *Eat Pray Love*, I've read many of Gilbert's works. I've studied the way she crafts her stories, how she meanders from one idea to the next holding our hands, gently pulling us along on the journey beside her. I've studied how she writes with a generosity in which she truly cares about us, urging us to become creative beings and pursue our passions.

When you find your writing icon, I urge you to spend time examining their work to discover their secret sauce. Make friends with your icon even if you never get to meet them.

When you find your writing icon, I urge you to spend time examining their work to discover their secret sauce. Make friends with your icon even if you never get to meet them.

I see clearly now that I'd neglected my friend, Liz, during my relationship (and likely many actual friends too). I'd not turned to my heroine for inspiration because I'd unwittingly made my lover my hero instead. He was a man at the top of his game in his field and I revered his work and talent.

Caught in the toxic comparison trap, instead of sharing my work with him, I hid it. He never showed much interest anyway, so it wasn't that hard to conceal. If, like me, your love-life kills your purpose to write, get out now or at the very least resolve to fix the problem. You've no time to waste.

Gilbert's book *Big Magic*, along with a host of other books on writing and creative living, was, in part, my inspiration for *Brave Women Write*. My aim was not to copy her work but to add to it and the extensive array of texts already available on writing.

There are literally thousands of books on creativity, artmaking, writing, story-telling and the like. I can guarantee you there is no book on your subject matter that has not been done before in some way. You must not use the excuse that someone else has already done it to back away from writing what calls you. Besides, no concept is ever fully original.

Original. It's an intriguing word. You might not think you are creative because you fear you're not 'original', that you might be seen as a poor imitation of others. However, 'original' does not mean your work has never been conceived of before. It is about going back to your source, the place where something begins, your origins. Originality is the culmination of your own unique life experience and learning. With this new understanding of originality, you are free to create unhindered by what others have written before you.

I'm also intrigued by Gilbert's life story and captivated by her continuous quest for love. The twists and turns of her romantic life remind me to accept only what will fill my heart and to never settle for a mere dabbler again. I've loved immersing myself in her interviews and articles and I've seen her live on stage where I contemplated every word she uttered. She's humble, irreverent, challenging and kind yet also flawed and messy—just like me and you.

Gilbert's words inspired me to take that writing sabbatical in France and to write *Unstuck in Provence*. I'm commonly asked, often with a smirk from the questioner, if this was my own *Eat Pray Love* experience. My response is always, 'that would have been wonderful but impossible. I was accompanied by my surly soon-to-be teenager who was quite the romantic handbrake'.

There are so many ways my heroine continues to influence and encourage me. Indeed she is but one of many. I need only look at my bookshelf to consider the many other authors, who unbeknown to them, have motivated me to pursue a writer's life and to write with more courage. Any time I need inspiration for a new idea or a new direction, they are right there calling me and willing me to persist.

Have you chosen your own writing icon yet? Do you have that one-of-a-kind writer you can study and learn from? Someone you can rely on to inspire you to stop doodling and start producing?

Reflection and Action

Who is your writing icon and why have you chosen them?

12. Your Own Cheer-Squad
On Writers' Groups

A writer's life can be a solitary one. You might have a well-formed idea and a goal to write a novel, a memoir or a book of poems. One day you commit to that goal, to roll up your sleeves and forge ahead. And the next day it hits you that you're all alone with your words. You're on a desert island with no way off and no one to rescue you. You have no choice but to do the work solo.

While I am alone, I'm not lonely. I've felt lonelier at large conferences and concerts and even in gatherings of close family and friends than I've ever felt writing. As each day goes by, as you keep practising, you'll find this too. You'll become more and more plugged into yourself and your words. You're neither lonely or alone, perhaps less than you've ever felt in your life—because your truest love and companion is right there with you.

That doesn't mean you remain on your desert island till you reach your goal. You'll need a life-raft to return to the mainland to regularly connect with other special people. You'll need a supportive group of humans to cheer you through to that fateful day when you type The End.

You'll need your own small team of writer friends each working on their own writing projects. Why not call it your *Brave Women Writers' Group* for starters?

Some years ago I began exploring the Slow Movement. It's a philosophy that advocates a culture shift towards reducing life's frenetic pace. It began as a protest in Rome in 1986 by Carlo Petri who rallied people against the opening of the fast-food restaurant, McDonalds. The gesture ultimately sparked the slow food movement.

> You'll need your own small team of writer friends each working on their own writing projects. Why not call it your Brave Women Writers' Group for starters?

The movement refutes the notion that faster is better. The slow philosophy doesn't advocate for life at a snail's pace. It promotes action at a mindful speed and emphasises quality over quantity.

An idea to start The Slow School of Business came to my mind. It would be a community for small business owners, professionals and freelancers who were dedicated to building purpose-driven businesses from their creative endeavours. In a world where fast-change, quick-profit and short-term thinking dominates, I wondered if we could apply the principles of the slow movement to capitalism and reduce the damage extreme forms of capitalism cause to people and the planet. I spent weeks alone researching the idea and designing the concept.

At some point, I knew I had to escape my self-imposed exile and test the merits of my idea on others. It started with a few casual conversations with creatives and business people at the co-working place I was working in called The Hub. Then I invited eight people in for my very first Deep Dinner in the communal kitchen. Everyone brought a dish and a bottle to share. There's nothing like fine food and wine to connect humans over subjects that really matter to them. There was nothing to lose and much to gain.

Over months, the school grew as more people heard about the dinners and wanted to participate and contribute. Before I knew it, we'd created a community of volunteers, supporters, facilitators and creatives showing up and sharing their knowledge and skills. Over three years, our community hosted more than one hundred classes and events with more than three thousand people in attendance at venues and restaurants all over Melbourne.

You can also apply my approach to building Slow School to your own writing project. While you'll spend a lot of time writing alone, you must also get out from behind your laptop and test your ideas with others as you make progress. Do not make the mistake of waiting until you type The End before you share your work. You need to find the first followers early, those who believe in you and your ideas as you write. That's how movements are made.

By the end of those three years, I'd come undone. I'd given my all to the community and burnt myself out in the process. While it had been a break-even exercise financially, it had been a break-down exercise in my energy. I came to a grinding halt. I couldn't see a way forward that would allow me to continue to lead the community and devote myself to my writing.

With immense sadness, the school closed its doors. Now four years later I can see that it was a worthy experiment and in some ways a significant success but that like all good things, it had come to its natural conclusion.

Together we made a small dent in the fast universe. The school gave birth to many creative endeavours that still exist today and many people still come together to collaborate on projects. This community also contributed to the production and publishing of *Conscious Marketing* and *The Purpose Project*.

Today four of those Slow School friends (Sandy McDonald, Kath Walters, Yamini Naidu and me) belong to my own writers' group along with Di Percy.

Kath, Di, Yamini and I began the group in February 2020. We each had a book in mind and a goal to write a first draft manuscript within ninety days following Kath's process. Each Monday we'd gather at my home, set our personal writing goals and then get down to work. We practiced the Pomodoro technique I mentioned earlier in this book. We'd then have lunch and share how we were tracking and where we needed help.

Just a month in, COVID hit. Harsh lockdowns put a halt to our little gatherings. Rather than give up, we continued meeting each week and writing together virtually. These virtual rendezvous kept us sane, connected and focused when the world had shut down.

My three friends achieved their goal and finished their first drafts in ninety days. Bravo! While I didn't finish my book, I ended up with three half-written manuscripts, the ones now informing this book. While I did the work of writing, I didn't achieve the common goal.

At some point during the ninety days, I confessed my dilemma and declared that I was confused as to which book was calling me to a conclusion. I had nothing but love and support from these women and they challenged me to make a choice. Yet still I couldn't make a decision. I was exasperated with myself and perhaps they were frustrated with me too but they never expressed it. Kath, Di and Yamini went on to publish their books soon afterwards. Me? Nothing.

At the beginning of 2021, we decided to take time off as a writers' group to focus on our paid work and businesses instead. It was during this time, as I was wallowing in grief at the end of love, that I lost all will to write.

But after that fateful turning-point conversation with my ex—when the idea for this book formed—I knew I needed help. 'This time I really do have a book to write in ninety days. I promise!' I wailed in an email to the clan. 'Can we please regroup?' We began again and so this book is now in your hands with thanks to these women.

Our writers' group continues to this day although the way we work together has evolved. We invited Sandy into the group and now gather online for an hour every Monday morning at eight o'clock. We're no longer focused on the ninety day target to write a book as we all have different goals. We each have ten minutes to share our progress, to pose a question or seek advice. Sometimes we'll read a piece of our work and receive feedback. Every six weeks or so, we spend a Friday together somewhere out of town in someone's home or in nature. We make deep human connection, write and offer and receive advice on our writing projects.

Soon after regrouping, Sandy posed the idea that we each write a piece on why we were writing our books for sharing at the following week's gathering. It was tough. I was on the verge of declining to read mine after the others had shared theirs. My words felt too raw and too embarrassing to speak aloud. Somehow, I gathered the courage and spluttered my way through.

I must write this book because women still live in a world men built for themselves and other men. Today, too many women have just two options. We must contort ourselves to the male model or parody the historical female form to dupe men into adoring us. In my case, and in my love-life, I took the second option. I hid an essential part of myself, my books and my writing, so he would not judge me, and therefore in my mind, love me. I lost my purpose to publish.

Even as a strong feminist with the most amazing array of feminist friends, I uncon-sciously subjugated myself to a man. I can see now the pattern recurs, not

> **You must find your own cheer-squad of women to will you to keep writing. A group of women to write with you, to hear your words and hold your hurt when you can't hold it alone.**

just in my life but in many women's. This book is my attempt at breaking that pattern. It's an effort to transform my sorrow and heartbreak into liberation through the power of writing and to show other women how to do the same.

As I uttered those last words, a silence settled over us. I felt heard and held. Such is the power of a writers' group.

You must find your own cheer-squad of women to will you to keep writing. A group of women to write with you, to hear your words and hold your hurt when you can't hold it alone. A group of women who will allow you to hold their pain in return. The right cheer-squad is out there for you. Initiate the search and it will find you.

Reflection and Action

Who will you invite to your writers' group
and how will you make it happen?

13. The Morning Pages
On Journaling

Morning pages changed my life. They're the tool for finding courage, the portal to my creativity, the flarepath through dark moments of despair.

My morning pages are three pages of freehand journaling written each day in bed before rising. I first discovered them in *The Artist's Way* by Julia Cameron, the text I referred to earlier in this book.

The writing is unfiltered. It's a pure (and very often impure) stream of thoughts, ideas and feelings around the events of my daily life, work, writing and relationships. Some of it is unintelligible and inane. But other parts are treasure—at least to me. What comes to mind ends up on the page, whether I like it or not.

Journals help me record my desires, express my gratitude, work through my grief and emotions and set plans for the future. One of the greatest gifts of journaling is its capacity to guide both big and small decisions. Often, I'll go to sleep at night posing a question and, in the morning, the answer miraculously appears in my journal. The words just seem to leap onto the page and lead me to my truth. Not always, but regularly enough to make the practice rewarding.

My journals are not fancy leather-bound volumes. Such ostentation would pressure me to produce a matching elegance and eloquence, contrary to their purpose. They're simple, inexpensive, lined wire-bound foolscap notebooks, so I can access one blank page at a time. I write with an equally inexpensive black ball-point gel pen that flows nicely across the page. It fits neatly in my hand and is perfect for my large and loopy cursive handwriting.

For me, handwriting is the only way to journal. I struggle to handwrite electronically although there are now many great online tools for just that purpose. As I spend so much time writing on my computer, handwriting is the perfect contrast. It allows deeper access to the recesses of my heart and mind that typing can't. If you're going to journal, experiment and discover what works best for you.

I distinguish between keeping a diary and using a journal. The first is more a factual record of events and experiences for future reference. I've never kept diaries myself but if you have, they'd be a great reference for that story-timelining exercise. Using a journal on the other hand is a more spiritual experience. It's my meditation, therapy and prayer all wrapped into one. It sets me up for the day.

> **Journals record my desires, express my gratitude, work through my grief and emotions and set plans for the future.**

I still recall the very first morning I started journaling. It was 6 September 2010, and my very first line was *These morning pages are going to be a drag and it's only day one.* Amusing.

You'll find this too. At first journaling feels really challenging. Negative self-talk and judgements appear as you first attempt to write. 'But I can't journal. I have nothing worth writing about. It seems so self-indulgent and self-centred. I don't have time for it. What if someone finds it and reads it? What if it brings to light that issue, that problem, that pain I've been avoiding for years?

Yet journaling, when done regularly, is the most powerful tool you may ever find for exploring emotions and healing grief. Day after day, as you write through the flotsam and jetsam, you will eventually dig up and reveal pathways towards truth.

If you haven't yet discovered journaling as an essential practice for life, here are a few reasons to burst through the excuses and the discomfort:

1. Journaling is your own psychologist.

While I'm a big fan of counsellors, therapists and mental health professionals, you already have a deep well of wisdom within you that's accessible through journaling. Free-form and continuous pen-to-paper journaling allows you to access that wisdom as it helps make the unconscious conscious. It reveals the questions you most need to ask yourself without you needing to rely on a therapist for the question. And very often it will result in an answer.

2. Journaling is available 24/7.

Journaling, unlike a counsellor, is available to you any time of day or night and just when you need it. In addition to establishing a morning journaling habit, carry your journal around with you and write in it any time no matter where you are: at your desk, in a café or on public transport to work. Any time you're experiencing overwhelming feelings, journal in that moment. It just might be all you need to get to the other side.

3. Journaling is a great tool for gatherings.

Journaling works well as the pre-cursor to a mindful discussion with others whether it's your family, your significant other, a team at work or your own writers' group. Together, determine the question you want to ask and allow everyone time for private, contemplative journaling before having each person share. It's a way to gain clarity of independent thought without being subjected to the influence of others and it ensures everyone is heard.

4. Journaling costs almost nothing.

The old saying, 'the best things in life are free' is so true. Unlike therapy, journaling is inexpensive. Whether you choose pen and paper or an online tool, it costs very little. I fill one notebook about every three months and use about a pen a month. I try to buy recycled paper notebooks which cost a bit more but reduce my environmental impact. Electronic notebooks allow you to write free-style and save your pages to the cloud.

> **Using a journal on the other hand is a more spiritual experience. It's my meditation, therapy and prayer all wrapped into one. It sets me up for the day.**

5. Journaling is the gateway to honesty.

Sometimes heartbreak and personal challenges are buried so deep inside you that they block your potential. Journaling brings awareness to these issues and a level of honesty with yourself that you may not be able to access through thinking alone. One of my favourite poets and modern-day philosophers, David Whyte, asks, 'What is the question you are not asking yourself? And what might life look like on the other side of that question?' Try journaling on that one morning.

6. Journaling helps you manifest your purpose and desires.

What is your purpose? Why are you here? What do you truly desire? What would your life be like if you chose to heal your hurt through writing? What would your daily life look and feel like as a writer? Journaling is the path to imagining what's possible for you, to create a vision for your life. Also, use your journal for creative endeavours other than the written word such as drawings, photographs, images, quotes and cards that inspire you towards purpose and creativity.

7. Journaling helps clear blocked emotions.

My therapist, Ishma Alvi, introduced me to the four hundred emotions humans can experience as I was dealing with my grief at the end. 'Feeling bad does not mean it *is* bad. Lean into it. What is it telling you?' she asked me. Most of us can only distinguish between feeling good or bad and happy or sad and angry. If our emotional vocabulary is so limited, we can't possibly know how to deal with our feelings. The underlying cause of sadness might be that you are lonely, alienated or unappreciated, for example. Journaling can help you identify the feeling and find your way to its root cause so you know how best to respond to it. An old Persian adage says, 'This too will pass'. Journaling helps you identify the feeling and work through it so that it, too, will dissolve in time.

8. Journaling helps you plan your day.

While I don't advocate using a journal as a to-do-list, it can be helpful for resolving questions like, 'What would make me feel fulfilled by the end of today? What would a great day look like? What promises should I make to myself today?' Journaling helps you imagine—and then create your best day. It helps you cement positive habits and of course it is the tool to help you put writing front and centre of the day's activities.

9. Journaling brings out the great creator in you.

Journaling gives you access to the deepest creative recesses of your heart and mind. You can even write a whole book in a journal, or as a journal if that's your wish. I've used journaling as the pathway to conceive new books, unfold plot lines and develop characters. With this book, I have used journaling each day to help me choose my next story. It's also a great tool to help you move through writer's block.

Some months ago, I did a stock-take of the journals gathering dust in my storage cupboard. Over ten years I'd written an estimated three million words in fifty journals. Astonishingly, I'd never re-read them. I never felt the urge to go backwards, only forwards.

> **Journaling is the path to imagining what's possible for you, to create a vision for your life.**

One morning I journaled about my journals. 'Why was I holding onto them? What use could they possibly be in the future? Should I destroy them? If so, why? If not, why not? If I did destroy them, what might be a fitting ending for them?'

Finally, by the end of three pages, I decided I would shred them. I couldn't imagine ever re-reading them or using them as material for future books. And if I should die unexpectedly, I would never want to burden Billy with their content or having to decide what to do with them.

But the main reason was that I wanted to release them, to let the last decade of my life go so I could move on with the next.

One dreary weekend, I dragged them out of storage and spread them all over the spare room. I trawled through them one by one. I didn't read every word as that would have been torturous. I just read random selections. It was both delightful and frightening: delightful to recall the fabulous occasions and recognise my personal growth, and frightening because right there in front of me were all the scribblings of the exquisite highs and the devastating lows of the relationship. I could see clearly how wrong it was for me and how much it had cost me. At moments I felt sick.

> **Journaling helps you imagine—and then create your best day.**

After skimming each journal, I removed the wire-binders and piled up the countless pages in three large cardboard boxes for the shredder.

I piled them onto on a trolley and wheeled them down to the recycling centre at the end of the street. A huge blue paper and cardboard shredding machine confronted me as I walked in. It was a hungry monster, at least four metres high and twice as wide.

A kind man with a wide-open smile greeted me. I shared the story behind the pages and what a big moment it was for me to let them go. He stepped up onto a hydraulic platform via a ladder and dumped them into the top of the shredder. He then stepped down and allowed me to step up so I could take a photo looking down on my pages. 'Thank you for the memories. It's time to say good-bye,' I whispered to myself as I stepped down.

In a contemplative and calm state, I stood by as the man turned on the machine to shred my pages. Once he'd finished, I stepped back onto the ladder to gaze down upon the empty cavity where my pages had once been to take another photo.

My pages have now moved onto their next life. I sometimes imagine little bits and pieces have found their way all over the world. And the two photos, entitled *Before & After,* hang framed in silver on my wall. Now whenever someone enquires about their significance, I have a story to tell. My whole being feels lighter for it too. It really was a letting go of the old so I could create anew.

I urge you to give journaling a try. Make time to do it, in bed each morning, on rising, or last thing before sleeping. Apparently it takes sixty-six days to form a new habit. Do your level best to make journaling your new habit.

Get started by journaling on one question a day. Do a Google search for some questions to journal on. Buy *The Artist's Way* or *The Purpose Project* for more than a hundred journaling questions. Start by journaling for one paragraph. Gradually increase it to a page, then two or three pages. Or set a timer for five minutes on the first day, then gradually increase it to thirty minutes per day over a few weeks.

If you can find the will to push through it and commit to it, I promise journaling will transform your day—and your life. Don't delay. Try it today.

Reflection and Action
What will your journaling routine look like
and when will you begin?

14. A Balancing Act
On Life Practices

As transformative as journaling is, at times it has a dark side. You can get stuck in your head on one train of thought and it can result in frustration rather than illumination. If this happens to you, don't give up. Notice it and take a break before continuing.

One morning, I was counting on my journal to reveal the next bead, but it was extremely resistant. So instead of pushing through, I stopped dead in my writing tracks.

The cawing crows outside my window urged me to down tools and pay attention, to just breathe and listen. Placing one hand on my heart, the other on my belly, I took a series of deep breaths and soon noticed magpies, bellbirds and a host of other unidentifiable birds calling me in to the brand-new day.

By turning my attention to the outside world for some time, I was eventually able to return to my inside world. I asked myself a new question. 'What story would be healing for me right now and what would be healing for my readers?' Returning to my journal, these words appeared from nowhere: *Lockdown. Mental health. Self-care.*

Till now, I'd quite deliberately avoided ruminating on the subjects of COVID, lockdowns and the pandemic that has altered our way of life, possibly forever. Writing has been a way to escape from it, a retreat into private normality and a time to forget the insanity outside.

Besides, this book was intended to help you heal your grief through the power of writing. What could a pandemic possibly have to do with it? On the one hand, nothing. And yet, outrageously, everything. For so many, this pandemic was (and continues to be) a great cause of sorrow and suffering.

At the time, our state of Victoria was enduring its sixth lockdown since the pandemic hit our shores and we had no certainty over when it would end. Our freedom was restricted. Mental-health issues escalated. It did immeasurable damage to our economy. People struggled in vast numbers, hundreds of thousands became ill—and thousands died. And still it persists.

On the other hand, the lockdown gave many of us the space to work out what, and who, really mattered to us. It gave us time to focus on the things we *could* do. It forced us to change the way we live within a new-world paradigm we could never have anticipated. We chose something more worthy for our lives than we ever might have imagined pre-pandemic.

> **Writing is one activity you can pursue almost without limit.**

Writing is one activity you can pursue almost without limit. You can change your life through the written word. When every day feels like Groundhog Day, when you can't leave home, whether that's due to lockdown or illness or family reasons, writing is the way forward. It's the way to soothe your soul and help yourself first so you can be of help to others.

Every one of my writers' group friends has attested to this. Writing during the pandemic saved them. The act of meeting each week online and talking about writing. The act of gathering to listen to the loveliness of each other's words and offering encouragement. The act of researching for writing. The act of turning average sentences into great sentences. Even the act of writing dead plain boring words. All of it made living in this uncertain world bearable.

And now, after a six-month writing drought then a return to writing every day, I know that for me, writing most positively improves my mental health, sense of peace and overall happiness. While I've always suspected this, now I know it for sure. I need writing like the air I breathe. Without it, I am a fish out of water, out of oxygen and dying a slow death. It's the ultimate practice in my suite of self-care practices.

However, it's not the only discipline.

Yoga. Reading. Swimming. Dancing. Bushwalks. Communing with nature. Meditation. Healthy eating. Limited alcohol. Music. Sleep. I employ these other self-care practices to complement my writing too. If I don't integrate them into my life alongside the work of writing, I lose balance and compromise my words.

If I over-imbibe over dinner, I risk delaying or even abandoning my writing the next morning. If I don't meditate, my head rules and my words lack heart. If I am too busy to engage with Mother Nature, I lose my purpose for writing at all.

All that said, you must not become obsessed with writing to the exclusion of all else. To be a brilliant writer, you must have at least a few other essential practices in your life, daily habits to devote yourself to alongside your work, conventions to bring out the best in you, so you can bring out the absolute best in your words.

Something euphoric and inexplicable happened around my self-care practice of swimming during the last lockdown in Victoria. It was tantamount to falling in love again. The pools were all closed and we were restricted from travelling more than five kilometres from home, making the beach out of bounds. However, the Yarra Birrarung river was just five hundred metres from home so at least I could be by the water, if not actually in it.

Once as I meandered along the river, I sat on my favourite meditation stone at an old swimming spot called Deep Rock. Watching a German Shepherd retrieve a stick, I lamented to the dog's owner, 'Oh to be a dog!' 'People swim here too now,' she responded with shock in her voice. 'There's a group of women swimming most days, can you believe it?'

Disbelieving yet hopeful, I raced home on a mission. Within seconds I was at my laptop posting a message on our local Facebook group asking if anyone knew these crazy and courageous women. Minutes later I received a response and some days later I was swimming in the river with my new friends, despite the water being a mere eight degrees Celsius.

To be a great writer, you must live a balanced life, one that includes other healthy activities and regular adventures—like river-swimming. It's vital to bring out the best in you, and therefore, the best in your words.

Now, every morning at dawn, the Yarra Birrarung calls. Nothing gets me out of bed faster than the thought of being immersed in water (no matter the temperature) with the Yarra Yabbies, the community of women I've come to love. Each morning as the sun rises, we greet each other, strip down to our swimmers and step gleefully down the rocks to the water's edge before sliding in one after the other.

It's like entering another world. At first my head remains above the water while the cold catches in my throat. The water is brown yet silky against my skin as I lose my land legs and morph into a mystical amphibian.

Breaststroke is perfect for river-swimming. With eyes at water level, I can take everything in. I look up to the native golden wattles and Yarra gums growing out of the rocky cliffs on the other side of the stream. Thousands of sweet-smelling golden flower heads from the wattles bob across the water's surface. It's like a starry night-sky. A pair of snow-white geese in the distance gather insects in the reeds, while a raft of black ducks glide by and attempt to herd us in to shore.

I try not to think too much about what might be below. I can sense the eels, carp and cod and all manner of creatures lurking beneath. Thank God they're invisible to me. I'm grateful to them for allowing me in and leaving me alone. Now and then, a small fish jumps out of the water for a quick peek at what lies above before plopping back home.

As we swim, joggers and walkers stop with looks of astonishment on their faces. They yell questions at us across the water. 'Is it cold? Is it clean? Is it safe?' And every so often, 'Can I join you?' Yelling back, we share our mobile numbers and ask them to text us their names to join our private WhatsApp group.

It's the way to soothe your soul and help yourself first so you can be of help to others.

On many mornings, a new swimmer arrives a little anxious yet thrilled at the prospect of brightening up their day. The shock and the joy on their faces as they submerge into the water is a delight to witness. By the end of the swim, this stranger has become a friend. Every day we are privileged to see one more person find healing in the great Yarra Birrarung.

For me, it's both a life-changing and life-affirming experience. It's a spiritual encounter, one that is as close to heaven as I can imagine I will ever get. I feel a part of Mother Nature, no longer apart from her. We are one.

There have been so many benefits to river-swimming. It made the monotonous lockdown days magical again. It was the liquid fuel required to write every day. It was the combination of wild water, wise women and writing that became a better prescription for depression than any drug—and it washed away my heartbreak.

It even gave rise to this poem:

River Love
I'd strolled beside you,
looked longingly at you,
wondered about you for years,
but I'd never truly known you.
Not like my lover or my mother.
All along I ignored your calls
to become one with you.
One day I was hurting so much
I turned to you for comfort.
I didn't know where else to go.
Soon I was submerged in you.
Even at eight degrees Celsius, you welcomed me in.
'Finally,' you whispered.
'You are here and we are one,
and our healing can begin.'
And every day I return so that
we might breathe life into each other.

Warning: Once you find your writing groove, you risk becoming obsessed. It can take over your life. You'll spend every waking moment plotting, planning and producing. Your life can become unbalanced and you might neglect the other self-care practices that ensure a well-rounded life. That's fine at times for short bursts when you must but it's not sustainable.

To be a great writer, you must live a balanced life, one that includes other healthy activities and regular adventures—like river-swimming. It's vital to bring out the best in you, and therefore, the best in your words.

Reflection and Action
What self-care practices will you commit to,
to bring out the best in you and your writing?

15. Three Trees
On Knowledge

Writers are seekers, explorers and way-showers. We chart new territory. We love discovering new ideas, new ways of thinking, new ways of expressing concepts. If we're not learning, we're not growing or expanding. We shrink inside and our words shrink with us.

Knowledge and know-how are what drive us and inform our writing. There are three trees of knowledge you might consider as you write: knowledge of the self, knowledge of your subject, knowledge of your craft.

1. Knowledge of the self.
Self-knowledge demands an understanding of what really matters to you, your beliefs, values and motives. The greater your self-knowledge, the greater your capacity for producing truly unique and provocative work. Your personality bursts through and your writing makes a statement the universe cannot ignore.

When I stepped out from behind those bars after my marriage, I had no idea what lay ahead. It was a huge step into the unknown and the beginning of real self-discovery. The single life, a new house, a large mortgage and the uncertainty of how to make a new business financially viable, would do that to anyone. Sometimes it's hard to be human. But at the same time, it's exhilarating.

One day I was a married employee and the next I was a single mother and business owner.

'You don't have the luxury of time to navel-gaze or cry yourself to sleep,' I would tell myself harshly if sorrow lurked around. 'Just get on with it, be a good mum, build this new business and begin again.' And so I did. If I had my time over, I'd tackle one component of my life differently. I'd give myself the time to fully face and feel the grief.

What I knew for sure was that I needed a new life utterly different to the previous one. It would not involve immediately re-partnering and creating some form of blended family or having to return to the corporate world. It had to be one that would offer freedom and allow me to be true to myself.

According to palliative care nurse, Bronnie Ware, in her best-selling book *The Top Five Regrets of the Dying*, the number one regret is 'wishing I'd had the courage to live a life true to myself, not the one others expected of me'.

I had to get to know myself in a way I'd not had the opportunity to before. The instruction curve was near-vertical. While I was hungry to learn new things, it was just as vital to unlearn the conditioning of my past. 'The first problem for all of us, men and women, is not to learn, but to unlearn,' said Gloria Steinem.

Here's a fun way to start unlearning. Try journaling on it. Review your timeline and write down the important people, events and institutions that had an impact on your life. Then without thinking too much or filtering the answers, write down one great thing you learnt and one limiting thing. From my mother I learnt . . . from my father I learnt . . . from my job I learnt . . . from the church I learnt . . . from school I learnt . . .

Think of everything and everyone who has influenced you. For example, from the church I learned the importance of having a faith but I also learned blind faith and the lesson to be like Eve. Now, Mother Earth is my faith, and I am a feminist like Lilith.

> **The greater your self-knowledge, the greater your capacity for producing truly unique and provocative work.**

This exercise helps you determine what you still need to unlearn and what you're curious to discover. It's a way to get to know yourself better, to clarify your beliefs and values so you may find your own unique writer's voice.

Knowledge of the self will give your words power and conviction. Your words become braver and bolder and you will care less about what others think.

2. Knowledge of your subject.

Sound knowledge of your subject is essential to feel and appear qualified and confident to write on a matter. Some of us are specialists in a specific field, dedicating our whole lives to it. Others are generalists who know much about many subjects but haven't narrowed our field of learning.

Neither of these particularly qualifies or disqualifies us to write on a topic. Generalist journalists are a great example of this. They tend to acquire just-in-time-knowledge through a deep-dive on a subject. On the other hand, specialists in a field might never achieve the desired wherewithal or will to write on their topic of passion.

Don't let your perceived lack of knowledge dictate your writing future. The critical point is to determine *what* you're going to write and *why* you must write it. From here you can develop a course of action to acquire the necessary knowledge on your chosen subject.

> **The critical point is to determine what you're going to write and why you must write it.**

As an aside, while you may be writing as a way to heal your grief, that doesn't mean you must devote your writing to the cause of the grief. In fact, not writing about the cause might just be a better cure for it. Just as this book has been a way to write through sorrow at the end of love, rather than making the book about the relationship itself.

Learning is about accessing, retaining and using knowledge to acquire wisdom. Knowledge is gained through personal experience, a formal education, informal tuition, research, observation and conversations.

We each have our own unique way of gathering knowledge. Some people prefer to learn solo as more textbook, theoretical or academic learners. Others learn better informally, in groups or through conversation and practical action. We learn by doing rather than studying. Discover which way works best for you and trust that one way of learning is no better than the other.

Recently, I wondered if there was a dating guide written for feminists of a certain age like me. It's not a book I'm willing to write but one I'd love to read. Anyone up for the challenge?

You couldn't write this book with any credibility unless you were that woman of a certain age open to dating. And if you did want to write this book, a great way to learn is through a practical, experimental approach.

Your own story would need to be at its heart. Then you would supplement your own knowledge by reading other books on the subject, subscribing to podcasts, attending singles' events, researching stories online and conducting interviews with women who are dating, both those who've met the love of their life and those who've met with disaster or have uproarious stories to share.

You could even set yourself a real-life experiment. Commit to putting yourself on all the dating sites and going on fifty-two dates in fifty-two weeks. Write one story per week which you might publish as a weekly blog that will become a book. Maybe you might just find 'the one', or even 'the many', depending on what you're up for. Which, of course, will lead to a sequel. While this is not something I'd do myself, it demonstrates how ideas, even extreme ones like this, can progress into works of imagination.

> **Do not risk becoming an over-learner at the expense of under-writing. As I've said, we learn most by writing.**

There are so many ways to gain knowledge on your subject matter. Be creative about it and make a game of it. It's guaranteed to give your words pizzaz and personality.

3. Knowledge of your craft.
Can you tell I'm a self-taught writer? I've no degree or formal qualifications in writing but I'm constantly learning more about the craft.

I have friends with undergraduate and master's degrees in writing who've never published a word outside the academic arena. For whatever reason, they've completed their course then firmly closed the lid on their writer's desk, turned the lock and dispatched the key. Maybe this book will get them searching for that key. I can but hope.

There is nothing like doing the work of writing to learn about writing. 'Write and you will learn—and heal,' is my motto.

You, too, must commit to learning more about the craft of writing. Read the top ten books from *Writing Down the Bones* by Natalie Goldberg to *On Writing* by Stephen King and *Bird by Bird* by Anne Lamott. Join the Australian Society of Authors and attend their courses. Attend writers' festivals and complete masterclasses with writing experts—in the flesh or online.

If you prefer more self-directed, informal learning, create your own free-range learning programme. Make it your own private Masters of Writing but if you're not so disciplined and you feel a formal university qualification is for you, do it. But please know that it is not essential to becoming a brave and brilliant writer.

The most enjoyable way to learn is to be a voracious reader. All genres. Fiction. Non-fiction. Short stories. Poems. Speeches. Articles. Blogs. History. Read with two intentions. The first, for pure enjoyment and the love of learning something new. The second, to study the constructs, grammar, language, narrative and vocabulary of good writing. Alternate between fiction and non-fiction to get some balance. When you come across a word you don't know, check the dictionary app on your phone to find its meaning and while you're at it check the 'word of the day' to expand your vocabulary.

I know one writer who insists on using a printed dictionary rather than an electronic app. He concedes it takes a little longer but says the benefits far outweigh the time saved. Aside from exercising his brain alphabetically, he takes joy in discovering new words or re-acquainting himself with old favourites during the search.

Becoming a great writer is akin to training for a marathon. If you've never run before in your life and you're twenty kilos overweight, you'd never just turn up at the start line on the day.

You'd set yourself a twelve-month goal to lose the weight and get fit. You'd research what runners eat and plan a healthy diet. You'd develop a training routine and block out the time in your diary. You'd enlist the support of all the people in your life that care. You'd find a buddy to train with and join you on the marathon. You'd join a local running group and find the fittest person there and ask her advice. You'd read everything you could on the subject and find a heroine for inspiration. You get the picture.

Treat your learning as a marathon. There is no overnight success, just daily practice as you work towards your writing goal. However, do not risk becoming an over-learner at the expense of under-writing. As I've said, we learn most by writing. Learn. Write. Learn. Write. Write. Write. And write some more.

Reflection and Action
Where are the gaps in your knowledge?
What do you need to do to improve it?

16. The Brick Wall
On Courage and Recommitting

One morning, after a sleepless night, I was still wide awake at five in the morning. I grabbed my journal to try and write through my exhaustion and this came out.

Today, I have no heart for my work. I'm at a vulnerable point. I'm at the same point where I abandoned my last three manuscripts. What if I abandon this one too? What if I don't become a finisher? I've hit a brick wall and I've no way to get over it.

It went on and on for a full page. My self-doubt and fear took over. The words had a hold of me and I had no control over them. You'll do this too as you journal. It's okay. Run with it and let the words roll. Get them out and trust the process.

At the top of the second page, I took a deep breath and suddenly the *Serenity Prayer* popped into my head, as it often does. 'God [insert the power of your choice here], grant me the serenity to accept the things I cannot change, the courage to change the things I can, and the wisdom to know the difference.' And before I knew it, I was writing about what it meant to me and what I could change and what I couldn't.

That word 'courage' in the prayer stayed with me, which then gave rise to the words of Maya Angelou, the American poet and civil rights activist: 'Courage is the most important of the virtues, because without it, no other virtue can be practiced consistently. You can practice any virtue erratically, but nothing consistently without courage.'

Can you see where your journaling might take you? From fear to courage in one page. From hopelessness to hopefulness and smashing through brick walls.

Courage is the pathway to so many virtues. There is no creativity without courage. Paradoxically, the more you create the more courageous you become. Creativity and courage are the perfect partners. You'll discover this for yourself the more you write.

The antonyms to courage are not fear and cowardice but comfort, conformity and compliance. We are born with courage but as life goes on, we lose it. When we were young, we sang, danced, made art and climbed trees. We didn't care what others thought. We didn't even know we were being courageous. It was our natural state. As we grew up, we lost our capacity for courage and those other boring *c* words took over instead.

The word 'courage' originates from the Old French word corage and the Latin word cor which means heart. Your most important work as a writer—and a woman—is to continuously return to your courageous roots, to write bravely and from your heart.

Over the years, I've learnt that courage does not mean taking reckless risks or giving everything up and starting over (as I've been wont to do). More often these days, I need the courage to stay, to see things through and sometimes, to do absolutely nothing.

I need the courage to surrender and let go, most particularly of the people and circumstances I can't change—just like the man I loved and our relationship.

Despite all this, my courage muscle needs strengthening from time to time. What about yours? Here's a little exercise to test your own courage muscle. Go back through your story timeline or consider the events in your life where you had to call on your courage. What happened? Who was there? Was there pain or pleasure on the other side? How did your life change?

Overall, on a scale of one to ten, with one being total lack of courage and ten being full of courage, how courageous are you? Are you happy with your score? If not, what acts of courage will help you ascend the ladder? And is there a story in all this? Is there something that must emerge?

> **The antonyms to courage are not fear and cowardice but comfort, conformity and compliance.**

A crisis of confidence like I had, is neither unnatural nor a bad omen. It keeps you humble. It gets you out of your own skin and into the skin of your reader. Humility, I find, is also a most important virtue with which to write.

If you hit a brick wall and fear not finishing, as I did, you must find a way, through journaling or other methods, to recover your courage and recommit yourself to your work. You should return to that commitment statement I urged you to write. Place it front and centre on your desk. Read it every time you sit down to write.

If Elizabeth Gilbert is my heroine, Leonard Cohen is my hero. He would be another person with a seat at that Deep Dinner. He's not the best writing companion, however, as his words are somewhat distracting and I find myself singing more than writing. Lucky you can't hear me, singing being a talent I was told I did not have as a child. Cruel, and never say never, I say.

Do you have a musician whose music and words you love so much you can't get enough of them? Brilliant! Study every word. Study every note. Study their life. They'll ignite your words. They just might be the perfect accompaniment to your work, if they're not too distracting like Cohen.

To keep finding the courage to turn up at the page no matter what. To keep writing forward into new frontiers. To not look back. To write until the very end— and to be a finisher.

It's sad to me that I did not discover Cohen until my forties. How the first twenty years of my adult life were Leonard-less is beyond me. People either love Leonard like a brother (or a lover) or they don't. 'Music to slit your wrists by,' are the sacrilegious words more than one pagan friend has uttered to me. Each to their own. Cohen inspires me to write. This book, for now. And perhaps poems and songs one day? Who knows?

I last saw Cohen when he was seventy-eight years old on his final tour of Australia. Sharply suited, trade-mark hat in hand, he sauntered onto the stage. A nod of the head, a mischievous twinkle in the eye, a few words of gratitude—and he was off. The air was electric. The crowd erupted. I might have even cried.

Humble and gracious, Cohen gave of himself to the end. He wasn't just sharing his songs with us. He was sharing his soul. He was in service to every single human being in the audience. It felt like he was singing just to me. To this day, it remains the most outstanding concert I've had the privilege of attending.

Cohen was a most courageous and dedicated artist. When I lose a little faith in my writing, I listen to the *Tower of Song* as a reminder to keep at it. The song is a statement about his commitment to the craft of song-writing. It pays homage to the courage of sticking with it through the bleakness.

In an interview in Q magazine in 1991, Cohen said, '*Tower of Song* is that place where the writer is stuck. For better or worse, you're in it. I've come this far down the line. I'm not going to turn around and become a forest ranger or a neurosurgeon. I'm a songwriter.'

Even as he was dying, Cohen was doing the work. His fourteenth album, *You Want it Darker* focuses on death, God and humour and it was released just seventeen days before he died. I imagine his work was his most perfect companion as he passed through to his next life.

Cohen died on my birthday in 2016. Seeing the news flash across my laptop screen, I stood up from my desk and walked outside to get away from the people in my office. Dazed and shaking, I shuffled around the block until I came to a park bench. I sat and rang my greatest Leonard-loving friend, Jenks. Together, we sobbed.

For six decades, Cohen committed himself to his art, to revealing his soul to the world through poetry and song. His timeless humanity touched our very core and his words will live on for evermore.

Tower of Song and the story of his life remind me to keep committed to my own work. To keep finding the courage to turn up at the page no matter what. To keep writing forward into new frontiers. To not look back. To write until the very end—and to be a finisher.

Reflection and Action

What will you do to keep your courage up
and recommit yourself to finishing?

17. Why? What? Who?
On Foundations

So, you have a big idea for your writing project and you're ready to begin. Great news and congratulations. But wait. Don't start yet. You must put down some foundations to your idea before hitting the keyboard or grasping the pen.

Before getting your writing underway, start by answering the three most important questions of *why*, *what* and *who*. *Why* are you writing? *What* are you writing? *Who* are you writing for?

In the beginning, still sad and washed up, it was all I could do to just get up and write what came to me each morning. The day by day, bead by bead approach was all I had in me. I didn't think much about these questions. You might find this too at first. That's okay. It's enough to be writing so don't worry.

Very soon after I began, however, I returned to these foundations and spent significant time writing answers to these questions. You should do this too. Firstly, because it's a duty of care to your readers and secondly, because it will prevent extensive reviews and even complete rewrites down the track.

1. Why are you writing this?
While shock tactics and statistics don't always work, maybe these will. It's widely known that eighty percent of people who start a book don't finish it and that of all the books finished, less than one percent end up published. I've been a victim of these statistics a few times and I don't want you to be one too.

The cleverest way I know to avoid becoming a statistic is to start with your *why*.

Very often we get stuck in the *what* and the *how* of our writing. We forget to ask *why* we want to achieve a writing goal in the first place. Yet understanding our *why* and continually returning to it is the secret to finishing. An unshakeable answer to *why* is our way through.

As a teacher of purpose and story-telling in the worlds of business and education, asking *why*, or the purpose of something (a human or an entity), is what I do. I define purpose as 'accomplishing something that is meaningful to you and of consequence to the world beyond yourself.'

That's the question you're answering. 'What am I here to write that is meaningful to me and will make a difference to the lives of my readers?' In the chapter on writers' groups, I share my own *why*. This is my anchor to return to when words elude me or I'm filled with self-doubt. There is nothing more vital than knowing *why* you must write.

> **The cleverest way I know to avoid becoming a statistic is to start with your why.**

I hear you ask: 'But can't I just write for the pure joy of it? Can't it just be for me? Do I have to try and fix other people's problems or even world problems with my words?' Yes, of course. Do it for sheer joy. That is a purpose, in and of, itself.

I promise, however, if you dig a little deeper, you'll find something you want to fix or change in the world with your writing. Find the small, quiet, private change or the big public 'burn-down-the-system' transformation you want to make. When you connect to this, you write for a purpose beyond yourself. Your words have greater power when you produce them in service to others.

The ultimate purpose of your work is to make people think, feel and act. So, ask yourself *why* you want to write. How does it change you? How does it change your readers' lives? My friend, Julie Gibson, told me that her friend left her miserable, long-term marriage after reading *Unstuck in Provence* and that she's never been happier. One more woman liberated. That's my purpose fulfilled right there.

So, write a list of all the reasons *why*. Make it thirty-three reasons *why*—one for each practice in this book. Start with the personal reasons: To heal my grief. To be a best-selling author. To break my writing drought. Then shift to the *why* outside yourself: To help my readers heal their grief. To help women write and share the stories they've always wanted to. To encourage women to be the change they wish to see in the world. And on it goes.

Then write two hundred words on your *why* to wrap it all up. Make it so powerful that you'd be willing to share it with a friend, your writing buddy or writers' group.

2. What are you writing?

Once you know your *why*, be open to how you answer the *what* question.

What are you writing? An essay. A non-fiction book. A series of short stories. A screenplay. A novel inspired by a true story. A book of poetry. A series of blogs.

You have many choices to fulfill your *what*. My own tendency is to opt for non-fiction books like this one. They are guides that weave in my own life stories. Others have described them as a cross between a self-help, memoir and how-to guide. My last two books were like this and now this one too. I've stayed within my writing comfort zone. Nevertheless, I shall finish and find the courage to write outside the zone next time.

On reflection, this book could have been a novel inspired by my true story. I could have fulfilled my *why* through fiction and achieved the same result—perhaps an even better outcome. One of the joys of writing fiction is that the reader will never know fact from fantasy. You can write without inhibition and with a wild imagination. You can write through your feelings to the other side with no obligation to write the truth.

Do not limit yourself. Go exploring the different ways and the various genres you could adopt that will allow you to respond most freely to your grief—and your *why*. Explore three options before deciding on one. Don't do what I did and stick to only what you know or the most obvious. Think big and be creative.

The other *what* questions you will want to consider are these. *What* is the one question you're answering for readers? *What* problem does it solve? *What* desire does it fulfil? Write about the problem or the desire at length and then summarise it into a few sentences.

> But a few days in, I realised I was writing for you. Women who want to heal and change their life with their story and words. Women who want to grow spiritually through it. Women who want to change the world with it. Women who are feminists and activists who want to remake the world.

Here's the answer to the *what* question for this book: 'I am writing a non-fiction guide that reveals my own stories and thirty-three practices for writing. It is for women with the desire to heal their grief through the power of writing and to make personal and planetary change. I will show them how to make writing a daily practice in their lives to get their idea out on the page and out into the world.'

3. Who are you writing for?

So now you know the *why* and the *what*, it's time to identify the *who*.

Initially, I had a vague idea this book would be for anyone who wanted to get better at story-telling and writing: corporate types, business owners, women, men, young, old, all genders, all ages, all races. I was writing for everyone which is the ultimate kiss of death for any work.

> **So, *who* do you hope will love reading your words as much as you love writing them?**

But a few days in, I realised I was writing for you. Women who want to heal and change their life with their story and words. Women who want to grow spiritually through it. Women who want to change the world with it. Women who are feminists and activists who want to remake the world. Old women. Young women. Courageous women. Compassionate women. Committed women.

I wrote a page-long reader avatar about you. From then on, I wrote my words through a new lens. They took shape for both me and you.

Before you begin, do the *who*. It will really make your words more potent and memorable from the get-go. *Who* is your reader? What can you assume about them? Why would your reader care? What are their lives like? What really matters to them? Who do they aspire to be?

Write about your reader in great detail. Give them a name. Describe their family situation, age, occupation and culture. Write about their beliefs and values, what makes them happy, what makes them sad and what keeps them awake at night. Your goal is to write them into your life—and your stories.

Make them your imaginary best friend. Or perhaps they're a real friend in your life already. Either way, each day, if you've the imagination for it, invite them to sit beside you, a ghostly companion to consult who wills you to do the work without saying a word. Imagine this person has a seat at your Deep Dinner.

So, *who* do you hope will love reading your words as much as you love writing them?

Take a break. Go for a walk among Mother Earth's bounties with your journal. Find a big, old, beautiful tree and sit at her base or climb into her loving arms. Write on the answers to these questions: '*Why* are you writing? *What* are you writing? *Who* are you writing for? And seek the wise counsel of your imaginary reader and even your ancestral elder while you're at it.

Write down all your thoughts on that big idea bubbling away in your heart and mind and why it needs to come to life. Don't stop. Write till you can write no more. Don't leave until every cell in your body is willing you to stop dreaming and start delivering.

Reflection and Action
Write fully on your *why*, *what* and *who*
then summarise it in one page.

18. And Now the *How*
On Planning

So now you have the foundations of your big idea. You're crystal clear on what you're here to write. You've not a doubt in your mind and you can't wait to begin. You've even blocked out the time in your diary to do the work.

Then BAM! A major distraction hits you between the eyes. An ailing parent needs you. An important, time-consuming client takes over your day. A family drama erupts and all of a sudden fate suspends your dream.

You could list one hundred obstacles that might stop you from getting started. Big and small. If it's helpful, go to your journal and capture them. List all the excuses to do anything else but write. Make sure you include TV and social media. Then rip out that page and burn it.

In my experience, most of our perceived excuses are not the root cause behind why we don't get started. The real excuse is that we don't know *how* to make it happen. We don't have a plan for our work. If you wrote that list of excuses, did it include 'I don't know *how* to do this'?

Like anything in life, when we don't know *how* to do something, we are tempted to give up and stick with what we know. We'll do anything to avoid the discomfort of being a novice.

I've written a lot in this book about courage and commitment. I come back to them time and again. Firstly, to remind myself to keep writing to the end and also to keep reminding you that without these qualities your words will flounder.

'Until one is committed, there is hesitancy, the chance to draw back, always ineffectiveness. Concerning all acts of initiative (and creation), there is one elementary truth the ignorance of which kills countless ideas and splendid plans: that the moment one definitely commits oneself, providence moves too.' The words are from the Scottish explorer and writer, William Hutchison Murray. (It's also a quote often attributed to Johann Wolfgang von Goethe, German playwright, novelist and poet.)

So, if you're committed to your idea and have the foundations of the *why, what* and the *who*, it's the *how* that will get you from empty page to typing The End. To shift from mere curiosity to serious commitment, it helps to have a splendid plan. A plan that keeps you focused on your goal. Then when life does happen, you will find yourself making the time for your words no matter what potential diversions present themselves.

A plan, coupled with a routine, will see you through.

Planning for a novel is very different to planning for a non-fiction book. For a novel you'll need to answer: What is the plot? Who are the characters? Who is the protagonist? Who is the antagonist? Where is the novel set? What events take place? Why would readers care? How many parts? How many chapters? Journaling is a great way to allow your plot and characters to unfold.

For a non-fiction book you'll need to answer: What is the single biggest question this book answers? What problem does it solve? How many parts and chapters will it have? What stories will you include? What do you want readers to do after reading the book? (Book you to speak, subscribe to your website, buy your online course?)

We'll do anything to avoid the discomfort of being a novice.

On a walk along the Yarra Birrarung one day, the idea for that dating guide for women of my generation popped into my head again. How would you bring such a book to life? Would you write it as a field guide or a novel? What would make you want to read this book if you were open to finding new love?

If you were to write it as a field guide, here are some ideas on how to approach it. It's a methodology that will work no matter what you're writing. See how it applies to your own big idea.

Write down the big idea. [A field guide for feminist women over fifty who are committed to actively dating in order to find a fulfilling, healthy, loving, inter-dependent, long-term relationship.]

Now set up a whiteboard or place a big sheet of white paper on a wall in your creative space. You might even make it a fixture. Grab a pile of sticky-notes and markers.

Go back through your life (or story-timeline) and pull out the names of the people you've loved romantically or dated. Choose the ones that had an impact. Write their names on a sticky-note. Under their name write down the defining experience or lesson you learnt from that relationship. Don't worry about what you'll write just yet or if it will be slanderous. You can avoid a potential lawsuit by changing names and details to de-identify them later.

Then write down chapter themes that come to mind on sticky-notes and place them on the whiteboard or paper. Self-love. Self-respect. Self-pleasure. Sex. Love. Beginnings. Endings. Romance. Desire. Loneliness. Dating apps. Dating do's. Dating don'ts. First dates. First appearances. Single-dom. Couple-dom. Polyamory. Queerness. Boundaries. Commitment. Feel free to add your own.

> **A plan, coupled with a routine, will see you through.**

Now share your book idea with your writers' group or a friend and ask them to contribute ideas for chapters. Once you've exhausted your list of potential chapters, start to group your sticky-notes and put them into some kind of order. See if they fall naturally into parts. Maybe like this: Single again. Dating again. Committing again.

Then think about the questions or points each of these chapters will answer and write them into a word document. Take that chapter on Endings. Perhaps it answers the questions of 'How do you know when it's over? How do you handle the end? How do you know when you are ready for new love?' Then put that sticky-note with the name of one of your old loves under that sticky-note. Now you have a chapter theme and a story to share.

Once you have a plan for the book, consider the content for each chapter. Will it be mainly your story woven throughout the book? Or will each chapter share the story of a different woman you might interview? What other books, references and research might you use to inform or supplement your words?

Here's another idea. Gather a group of women who fit your *who*. Ask them over for a Deep Dinner, share your idea and have some questions prepared to get the conversation started. Be sure to reassure them that 'what's said in the room stays in the room' and is not to be shared outside. Begin by sharing your own most revealing story. This will warm up the group and reassure them that they're in a safe and trust-worthy space. Ask them to share their most poignant stories. See what comes up.

You'll no doubt hear many revealing, heart-breaking and hilarious stories. Make a note of which stories might be worth exploring further for your book. At this point, your job is only to research and observe to gain more clarity. Don't make any promises yet about interviewing them or writing their story. I have found this has got me into hot water in the past. I've interviewed people only to find their story doesn't have a place in my book or the book I thought I was writing ends up being shelved. This can disappoint you both. You are in research mode only as you work out the *how*. Be curious. Enjoy the process.

You have a structure and a plan. You have your sticky-notes now in some kind of order to support your workflow. Now you're ready to commit yourself to getting the words onto the page. This is where that chapter on routine comes in handy.

Determine how many words you will write per chapter—five hundred or one thousand maybe? Then determine how many words you can write at each sitting, say between one hundred and five hundred? Then work out how many hours you have each week to write. Set yourself a daily, weekly and monthly goal and an end date. Block out weekends or whole weeks in your diary and remove yourself from the rat-race for a while.

Now when life deals up potential distractions, they'll happen around your writing instead of taking it over. You won't let them railroad your words because now you have a plan. And you know you can do it.

Note: I don't always follow this approach but have used it for most of my writing projects. If it feels a little heady or linear to you, start by writing what enters your heart each day and allow the structure to unfold as it's meant to.

Reflection and Action

How will you bring your big idea to life?
Develop a plan and a routine for it.

19. My Top Seven
On Writing Skills

I often repeat myself in this book. There's a method to my madness. You might find it annoying. That's okay. Dig into the cause of that annoyance. Is it me or is it you? Repetition is the secret to rewiring your brain and resetting your inner dialogue so you can remove your blocks to free the writer within.

Here are some of the blocks you might encounter:

You don't have a big enough *why* to write.
You don't have a goal, plan or routine.
You don't have a supportive partner or family.
You don't have other writers or a community for support.
You are scared of judgement and ridicule from readers.
You compare yourself to others and lack confidence.
You are not madly, hotly in love with your writing idea.
You think you don't have the skills to write.

And on the list goes.

That last one is a big reason why many of us don't write. We feel we don't have the technical aptitude to write well. I've already shared the importance of acquiring knowledge of the craft of writing in chapter fifteen, *Three trees*. Gaining this knowledge is a life-long process. But here are my top seven technical tips to get you started.

Note: These tips cover the art and science of writing, not the art of story-telling. More to come on story-telling in further chapters.

1. Write to learn.
No doubt you already knew this was going to be my first tip. I've said it over and over. There is nothing like doing the work of writing to get better at it. To improve at anything, whether it's parenting, taekwondo or the ukulele, practice is all. However, when it comes to writing (and many other creative pursuits) we believe we have to be perfect at it to be worthy of even making a start. Don't make this mistake. Be prepared to be an apprentice. Be willing to be perfectly imperfect. Just write.

An old friend of mine recently shared he'd been writing a book for ten years and that he was writing every day but with no end in sight. When I enquired what the book was about, he said, 'I'm not sure anymore but I'm having a hell of a lot of fun writing it!' We both laughed aloud. 'How wonderful,' I exclaimed. 'At least you're loving it and getting good at writing even if no one will ever read your words.' Write and you will learn.

2. At first, write your words straight.
Here's a quote my editor and writer-friend, Roger McDonald, loves. It's a maxim many journalists live by. It's from American author and cartoonist, James Thurber: 'Don't get it right, get it written.'

> Repetition is the secret to rewiring your brain and resetting your inner dialogue so you can remove your blocks to free the writer within.

You must be willing to do this, to just get the words down. Write the words that immediately come to you. Don't filter them. Don't worry if they're plain, dull and boring. Just get them out. Write the sentence 'the cat sat on the mat' or 'I walked with my son down to the beach to look at the waves,' if that's what your story is about. Don't worry that they're as simple as a first-grader's words. Have a giggle.

Then just write another sentence, and another and another. Get to one hundred words then one thousand words and keep going. Write the words straight and don't worry that they're not great. Write like no one will ever read them. Do not review and edit them as you go. Pour your words onto the page. If you do nothing else, this is it. When you reach your goal, shut your laptop and pat yourself on the back. Do not review your words. Yet.

3. Later, make your words great.
There will come a time, however, when you must turn those straight words into great words. Do this after one page, a whole chapter or after

the first draft manuscript is complete. As I was writing the first draft of this book, I just focused on my goal to finish the manuscript within ninety days, always going forwards never backwards. You might decide this is the way for you too or you might turn every thousand words from straight to great. This might help you write the next thousand words better the first time round.

When you're ready, take that sentence 'I walked with my son down to the beach to look at the waves' and find more interesting words. Think about your son. What's his name? How old is he? Use a thesaurus. 'Walked' becomes 'trudged'. 'Beach' turns into 'foreshore'. 'Look' is now 'scan'.

'My teenage-son Jack seized my hand. We trudged down to the foreshore to scan the waves.' It's now richer and more compelling. You now have a boy your readers want to get to know. They're left wondering why Jack and his Mum trudged rather than ambled or raced to scan the waves. You have two short punchy sentences instead of one dull sentence.

Write the words straight and don't worry that they're not great. Write like no one will ever read them. Do not review and edit them as you go.

To achieve this, make your thesaurus and dictionary your constant companions.

4. Every word must earn its place.
This tip is from my exceptionally talented writer-friend, Sandy McDonald. Most of us are a bit verbose with our writing. We use too many superfluous words. We overuse words and lose our reader in the process. So how might you eliminate the words you don't need? Sandy suggests removing most adverbs or words that end in 'ly'. She, and all the great writers to whom we return, believe diverse nouns and verbs should do the heavy work. Adverbs dilute them.

Read the first sentence of the preceding paragraph. Is that word 'exceptionally' of any value? Sandy says 'no'. 'This tip is from my talented writer-friend Sandy,' is sufficient. And even the sentence following it, 'Most of us are a bit verbose with our writing.' Change that to read, 'We're prone to verbosity.' You've now turned an average ten-word sentence into a four-word power statement.

A few years ago, I recorded eight short videos for an online course. It wasn't until I watched the videos later that I noticed my overuse of the word 'actually'. Of all the 'ly' words, this one is most useless. Remove it and see how it improves your work. You might not have a problem with the word but I guarantee you'll find others you overuse. Notice them as you write. Do a search of your document and remove them. Every word must earn its place.

5. The shorter the better.

> Words have the power to either build bridges between you and your reader or destroy them. Always try to build a bridge.

That's the tip from Roy Peter Clark, author of *How to Write Short* and my business book coach and friend, Kath Walters. We're referring to the length of a sentence, not your hemline, although we're all for short skirts. Short sentences have a place but you don't want your work to read like a marketing brochure. Long sentences work too. They're perfect if they take you along on the ride to the end. Play with the length of your sentences. Some short. Some long. Some in-between. Play with your hemline while you're at it.

I'm a lover of short sentences as you've no doubt noticed. However, for me, the jury is out on this tip. I am divided over it. I don't pay attention to the length of a sentence as I'm writing (or reading) but to the words and the sentiments within the sentence. Long, crawling, well-crafted sentences can take you on a journey and become a story in themselves. However, in the beginning, just get your words out. Don't worry about the length of your sentences. Shorten them later if it feels right.

6. Use simple words.

I've many friends with PhDs under their belts. I revere their intellect and ability to research and write on subjects I'll never comprehend. Their words hold weight for the world they operate in but they often don't feel accessible to me. A chasm yawns between my writing style and the writing world of most PhD candidates.

I sometimes find myself stuck in the comparison trap, doubting my own intellect and the intelligence of my words. However, intellect and intelligence are not the same thing. Intellect involves reasoning and understanding abstract matters. Intelligence is the acquisition and application of knowledge and skills.

My goal is to make my words as intelligent and accessible as possible. I use simple words, not terms that have readers reaching for the dictionary at every sentence. I don't, however, suggest you dumb-down your writing. It's far more challenging to enliven your work with simple yet evocative prose. It's harder to be non-intellectual and appeal to all.

Words have the power to either build bridges between you and your reader, or destroy them. Always try to build a bridge.

7. Be descriptive.

Turn flowers into pansies and transport your reader into their grandmother's garden. Change car to FJ Holden and carry them back to their childhood. Convert pastry into pain au chocolat and convey them to France. That last description takes me back to Aix-en-Provence and the café where Billy and I ate our very first croissant. Descriptive words release your reader into their own life stories and, of course, yours too.

Add adjectives wherever possible, but don't overdo them. Turn the pansies into baby-pink pansies. Turn FJ Holden into a decrepit FJ Holden or an immaculate FJ Holden or a rusted-out FJ Holden. Turn pain au chocolat into a melt-in-the-mouth chocolate croissant.

Try to engage all the senses. Ask yourself what you want your reader to taste, touch, feel, see, hear or sense. And ask yourself what you want them to do. Make your pain au chocolat so enticing that they snatch up your book, dash to a café and devour both a croissant and your words. The more descriptive you are, the more your reader will immerse themselves in your story. You'll have them eating out of the palm of your hands.

There's seven short tips to get you started straight away. Don't delay. Perhaps you have a piece of writing that needs a spruce-up. Save your straight copy, then write a better version. Be ruthless as you apply these principles. Then read the 'before' and 'after' and see the difference. Then keep writing. Don't stop.

Reflection and Action
Take your big idea, write one thousand words straight,
then go back and apply these tips.

20. Bring Your *Why* to Work
On Writing For Work

I revered Mr Gould, my maths teacher at high school. He was devoted to his work and every one of his students, no matter our abilities. Because of this, he inspired me to pay attention, work hard and do my absolute best. Mr Gould was the reason I was good at maths even though I had no love for the subject. And he was the reason I chose a banking career—despite having little interest in the world of finance.

For me, banking was an occupation, never my vocation. An occupation is a job you get paid for. A vocation on the other hand, is a calling. It comes from the word 'invocation' meaning it is a summons or appeal to the divine. Kahlil Gibran, the Lebanese-American poet, philosopher and author of *The Prophet* wrote, 'when you are born, your work is placed in your heart.' He was saying that you were born for a vocation.

I was not born to be a banker. In fact, I recall at a very young age, announcing to my family and friends that I wanted to become a teacher. Somehow, no one kept me to my promise. I ignored the work that had been placed in my heart at birth and fell into banking instead.

I'll never forget the day I left my twenty-year finance career in 2001 to start my own business. It was scary leaving behind the security of the corporate world and a regular income, yet it led me to my vocation as a teacher and now—a writer. Perhaps I needed to toil in an occupation before I could fulfill my vocation?

In hindsight however, I didn't need to leave my banking job to explore my calling. I could have held an occupation by day and pursued a vocation by night—and even blended the two. I could have been a banker, a teacher and a writer. I could have brought my penultimate *why* for writing, right into my work.

Are you working in an occupation or a vocation? If you're in a vocation, kudos to you. If you're in an occupation, my advice is not to quit your day job for your craft just yet. Experiment by bringing your *why* to work first. Work is the perfect place to practise being a better, braver, bolder writer—and to get paid for it.

Every workplace needs a whole lot more love in their written and spoken communications. Your enlivened words can make someone's day happier and brighter. They have the power to bring healing to the workplace and to your co-workers' lives beyond work. Imagine the difference we'd make if the writers among us amped up the love through our words at work.

In addition to the tips from the previous chapter, here are some tips to improve your workplace writing and make a positive impact:

1. Be human.
We've stripped workplace writing and communication of all humanity. We write to fit the dominant get-stuff-done culture. Short. Sharp. Get-to-the-point. Directive. Robotic. Our writing has lost its kindness, friendliness and empathy.

Our words most often never meet people's longing for belonging and connection at work. They only add to our disconnection and isolation from each other. And now, as so many of us are working remotely, we need words that connect us more than ever. Next time you receive a short, sharp email that lacks any sense of care, do your utmost to make the response warm, kind and generous. Always be human. You'll be surprised at what comes back.

> **If you're in a vocation, kudos to you. If you're in an occupation, my advice is not to quit your day job for your craft just yet. Experiment by bringing your why to work first.**

2. Adopt a writing personality.
We all have something unique about our personality that defines us. What are the distinct characteristics you have that you'd like to bring to your writing? Ask your co-workers what they love most about you and then infuse that quality as much as you can into your writing. Claim your style and personality and bring it to your words at work.

I have a business colleague with dyslexia whom I'd describe as bold and challenging yet friendly. He plays a game with his emails and requests people to limit their emails to one hundred words and three sentences if they want a response.

So, what's your personality? Cheeky? Kind? Humorous? Warm? Accessible? Challenging? Playful? I like to think my personality is warm, irreverent and brave in equal measures and so I try to write to those qualities in both my work correspondence and books.

3. Use loving language.
The corporate world is filled with war-like words that unconsciously destroy or damage our enthusiasm. Deadline. Competition. Execution. Trenches. Targets. Frontline. Coalface. Think about the words you use at work. Challenge the common and unquestioned use of words. Look up their etymology and assess if they're harmful or healing. Create your own list and replace those words of war with words of love.

Our words most often never meet people's longing for belonging and connection at work.

My least favourite corporate word is 'deadline', used as a term for setting a date or time for completion of a task. Its etymology shows it originated from the American Civil War as a warning to prisoners that if they crossed a designated line, they'd be shot. We use that word every day in business and it just doesn't make sense. If you took it literally, we'd kill the person who meets their target instead of rewarding them. What about using 'lifeline' instead? The day the goal is achieved, we get to breathe and have a life again. Phew.

4. Avoid weasel words.
You've probably heard of the term weasel words and the book *Watson's Dictionary of Weasel Words* by Don Watson. Watson was former Australian Prime Minister, Paul Keating's political adviser and speechwriter and is the author of many successful books. A good thesaurus and dictionary helps writers and speechmakers avoid using words and phrases that have become clichés and sidestep language that hides the truth. I can think of many a politician who could do with this book.

I recall seeing Watson speak many years ago. He shared an amusing story around the language of former Australian Prime Minister, John Howard, and his commitment to his 'core' promises, thereby implying that his other promises were 'non-core', leaving him without obligation to keep them. How a promise can be anything other than a promise is beyond me. Next time you watch the news, note the language politicians use. They say a lot without saying, or promising, very much at all. Avoid weasel words.

5. Tell a story.

Never miss the opportunity to tell stories in your communications at work. They are bridge-builders between you and your peers. Even if you have hardcore statistics, facts and research to disseminate, tell a story to illustrate why they're important. Statistics fuelled by stories make your message stick.

Imagine you're a school principal and you're sending staff an email from home after school. You have some bad news to share with your teachers. Start with: 'As I sat down to write this email tonight, my four-year-old, Ivy, climbed up on my lap . . .' End the email with what happened with Ivy. 'PS: Ivy is very tired but patiently waited for me to finish while playing with our Cocker Spaniel, Rusty, under my desk. Now we're making tacos for dinner. See you tomorrow.'

Stories create trust and connection. They invite people into your life and they encourage the recipient to share their stories too. They're the quickest way to each other's heart.

6. Watch unconscious bias and be inclusive.

Unconscious bias is all about unconscious favouritism towards, or prejudice against, people of a particular ethnicity, gender or social group which influences our actions, decisions or perceptions. We all possess unconscious bias within us and are prejudiced in some way, shape or form.

Jargon, acronyms, complicated words and inaccessible language contribute to a culture of divisiveness and exclusion at work. We have the power to eliminate bias by considering every person who will be the recipient of our words, not just the few who are like us. Making words and language simple and understandable breaks down barriers and connects people. They eliminate the likelihood of unconscious bias in our workplace. Always try to be inclusive with your words.

7. Make your emails matter.

According to Statista, we send over 333 billion emails around the world each day. They must be one of the most over-used and disliked forms of communication—at least for anyone over the age of thirty. I know younger generations are opting out of email in favour of instant messaging. Improving your email prowess has so many benefits for your day to day communications. And it will help you improve all other forms of communication too.

Give your email the personal touch. Reveal something of yourself. What matters to you. Make people laugh. Tell a little joke. Include a funny YouTube clip. Include a warm greeting. Eliminate long jargon-like legal disclaimers if possible. Include your picture and signature on your sign-off. Make your emails memorable so that people look forward to receiving them, reading them and responding. Email is a perfect way to invite people to peek at your humanity. Bring your work to life by bringing life to your words at work.

So, instead of just using your new-found writing talents for your private masterpiece, why not create masterpieces at work every time you write? Show your co-workers and leaders what you've got. You never know where it might lead.

You don't have to ask for permission. Dive in and see what happens. Infuse your workplace with creative writing. You might just find some other closet writers at work to join you. Perhaps even start your own writers' group at work? Make a game of it. Start a movement.

Do a writing stock-take. Make a list of all the important things you write for work. Emails. Speeches. Reports. Proposals. Brochures. LinkedIn profiles. Newsletters. Contracts. Financial reports. School reports.

Choose the one document that might be a game-changer if you were to excel at writing it. And then research how to become a master at it. Practise for five minutes daily for sixty-six days until you sparkle.

I do this often with my LinkedIn profile. Recently I spent half a day researching the latest on how to write them, then I rewrote my own and sought feedback from my writers' group, asking 'Does it say what I do? Does it say how I help? Am I credible? What's one way to improve it?' It's a work-in-progress but it gets better every time I review and polish it.

Next, I'm moving onto emails. I admit, I'm a lazy email writer. It's my Achilles Heel. So, my focus for the next sixty-six days is taking a dose of my own medicine and injecting more clarity and personality into them. Time after time, we teach what we most need to learn.

> **Email is a perfect way to invite people to peek at your humanity. Bring your work to life by bringing life to your work—and your words.**

So, bring your writing powers to work. See where it takes you. It will make a positive impact in so many ways. For your workplace. For your peers. And, of course, for your private work of art.

Reflection and Action

Choose the one component of writing that would be a game-changer at work if you gave it some serious attention. Don't delay.

21. The Quest Awaits
On The Hero's Journey

Joseph Campbell was an American professor who worked in comparative mythology and literature. He was the man behind the popular Hero's Journey monomyth and author of *The Hero with a Thousand Faces*. Campbell specialised in applying psychology to the lessons of myths and fairy tales and their relevance to modern day life.

I first learnt of his work when a friend recommended watching *Finding Joe,* a documentary and exploration of the mythologists' studies and the impact it still has on our culture today. The journey is a common narrative archetype many story-tellers, writers and filmmakers follow.

It offers a story template of the hero who is called to adventure, leaves home, overcomes adversity to learn a lesson and returns home transformed by his newfound knowledge. It describes a journey from the known through the unknown and back to the known and lays out the path to self-knowledge and self-actualisation.

Campbell outlines seventeen phases of the myth within three major stages: The Departure, where the hero leaves the familiar world behind; The Initiation, where the hero learns to navigate the unfamiliar world; and The Return, where they make their way home.

You'll see this narrative in many of today's famous books and movies such as the *Matrix*, *To Kill a Mockingbird*, *Lion King* and the *Harry Potter* series. You can also see it in the lives of many religious and historical figures: Buddha, Jesus, Mohammed, Martin Luther-King, Nelson Mandela and others. You can even apply it to today's entrepreneurs and visionaries and their quests to solve the world's most pressing problems.

The journey is a narrative arc that describes a story's full progression from beginning to end. From riches to rags and back to riches again.

From rise to fall and rise again. From happy-hearted to broken-hearted and back once more.

I've reflected a lot on the hero's journey narrative and taken some creative licence to modify it to make it more reflective of modern society and all genders, not just males. It's made it more useful to me in analysing my own life stories. Perhaps you'll find it useful too.

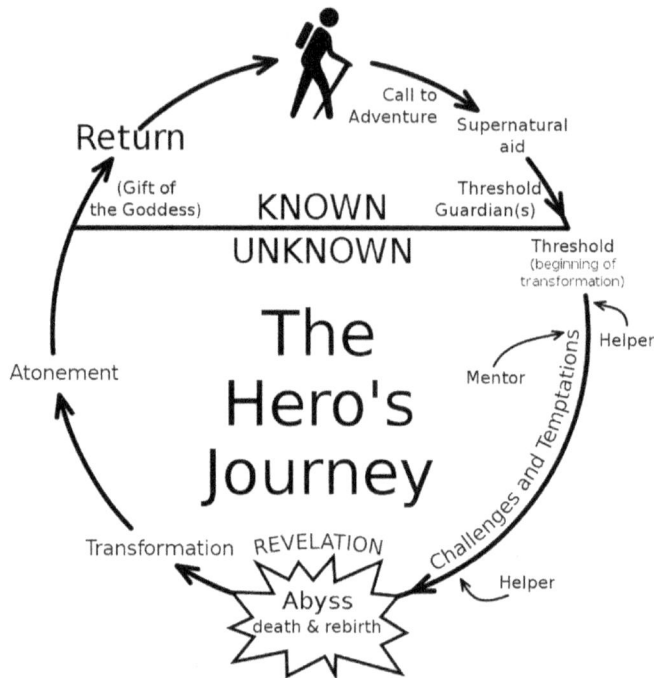

Campbell, Joseph, *The Hero with a Thousand Faces*. (Novato: New World Library, 2008)

Departure
1. The call to adventure: Something or someone interrupts your life and presents a challenge to be overcome. Or an opportunity presents itself and you must make a choice.
2. The refusal of the call: You are, at first, reluctant to take the call and to step out of your familiar territory. You must weigh up the consequences of taking, or not taking, the call to adventure.
3. Supernatural aid: You encounter a mentor, a wise person who advises, guides and helps prepare you for the adventure.

4. Crossing the threshold: You make the decision and embark on your adventure.
5. Belly of the whale: You cross the point of no return after encountering your first major obstacle.

Initiation

6. The road of trials: You must go through a series of trials and tribulations to begin your transformation. You fail at least once, if not more.
7. The meeting with the Goddess [or as I describe it . . . meeting your allies]: You meet one or more guides or mentors who willingly support you and help you continue the journey.
8. Woman as temptress [or as I describe it . . . love as temptation]: You're tempted to abandon your quest because you're distracted by a love interest—not only romantic but the temptations of fame and wealth.
9. Atonement with the father [or as I describe it . . . confronting the oppressor]: You finally understand the real reason for your journey which is to confront the powers that have ruled your life till now. This is a turning point. All steps before this have brought you to this realisation.
10. Apotheosis: You're at the pinnacle. You have an epiphany that provides a profound understanding of your purpose and your abilities and what you're being called to do with your life.
11. The ultimate boon: You have achieved the goal that you set out to accomplish and fulfilled the calling that inspired you in the first place.

Return

12. Refusal of the return: You may feel reluctant to return to your ordinary life if you've been successful on your quest.
13. The magic flight: You must escape with the object of your quest and fight off those who might try to reclaim it or attempt to prevent your return home.
14. Rescue from without: Like the meeting with your love interest in step eight, you encounter someone who may rescue you and journey with you home.
15. The crossing of the return threshold: You make a successful return to the ordinary world.
16. Mastery of the two worlds: You achieve a balance between who you were before the adventure and who you are now. You balance your material and your spiritual worlds.

17. Freedom to live: You are at peace with your life and the fulfilment of your purpose.

Writing this was revelatory as I considered the various journeys of my own life. What about you? Could you think of times in your life where the hero's journey has played out? Are you compelled to take the journey again? Or are you already on the journey at this moment?

Do not compare your journey to the Hollywood blockbusters or the stories of other famous people who've conquered devastating tragedies or achieved giddying heights. I've already written that comparison is an unproductive exercise and the thief of creative joy. Dig into your own journey, love it and own it. Use the model as a way to make sense of your stories and to inspire your story-telling and writing, whether fiction or non-fiction.

In 2010, Billy and I were living in the beachside suburb of Coogee, Sydney. In the early morning of 17 May, I received what I now consider to be my own 'call to adventure'. I was in that blissful, semi-conscious, sleepy state just before you awake. I sat bolt upright in bed and spoke out loud the words, 'let's move to Melbourne'. A vision had entered my heart and mind overnight and had tumbled out of my mouth.

Billy was fast asleep as I leapt out of bed, dressed and marched down to the cliff tops. I needed to fill my lungs with cool sea-air to become fully awake and know if the vision was a flight of fantasy or something more serious. Sitting on a boulder looking out at the ocean, I asked myself why?

We humans are on a constant quest to make the unfamiliar familiar, the uncertain certain, and the uncomfortable comfortable again.

Because my son needs his father—who lives in Melbourne—to be in his daily life. And I feel stuck. I feel stuck financially. I feel stuck in a business I'm no longer passionate about. I feel stuck in a monotonous daily routine. It hurts and I need to get unstuck. I need an adventure.

'Life is either a great adventure or nothing,' wrote Helen Keller, the blind American author and civil rights activist. As I strode home, I'd made the decision to heed the call. As soon as Billy was at school, I phoned his father to let him know. He was delighted and offered to do what he could to make the transition as smooth as possible.

But, it seemed, this was only the first decision. Five days later, another eclipsed it—the resolution to take a long detour via France. Intuition and instinct took over once I'd made the decision. I had to trust that I was making a good choice, not just for me, but for Billy too.

If I were to apply the hero's journey concept to this experience, I'd say The Departure was the ninety days it took from choosing to take the call to adventure to embarking for Paris. Leaving everyone we loved and everything we knew behind was our Belly of the Whale. The Initiation describes the whole sabbatical in France to a tee. As fabulous as it appeared to our friends and family back home, over and over we faced the Road of Trials in a country where we didn't know anyone and couldn't speak the language.

> **As a writer, you take the call to adventure every time you sit down to write.**

Then came The Return home which began on our last day in France on 1 January 2011 with my manuscript *Unstuck in Provence* on my laptop. It took some time to settle back in Australia in a new city and to re-establish a new home and business. There have been many smaller journeys since.

We humans are on a constant quest to make the unfamiliar familiar, the uncertain certain and the uncomfortable comfortable again. If anything has proven the need to accept that life will always be a continuous hero's journey, it's the pandemic. We've all been collectively thrust into a journey without choosing it and it's taken us into unknown territory. I get the feeling we'll never return to the home we once knew which is why we must each heed the call to our own personal hero's journey.

You might be able to identify many departures from the familiar to traverse the strange and the uncomfortable, to discover anew and learn a lesson before returning home to a place of reconciliation and acceptance.

It seems that our lives are filled with one hero's journey after another —big, small and somewhere in between. The idea that we're always being called to adventure and thereby achieving ever greater levels of enlightenment feels good to me, almost like a spiral of ever-growing self-knowledge and self-actualisation.

Divorce. Redundancy. Ill health. Bankruptcy. Death. They all cause grief. And these phenomena force us to take the journey. We have no choice but to search and rebuild. Each one changes our life in some way.

I'm most intrigued, however, with the idea of choosing to take the journey when there is nothing life-shattering occurring or when you have a simple desire to write. Nonetheless, you know there's something else out there for you. You wonder, 'is this all there is to life? Is there something more for me?'

It's tougher to make the choice in the midst of a general malaise, an air of discontent, a sense that life is dull and grey or a restlessness that won't go away. This is where the hero's journey comes into its own. It calls you to be honest with yourself, acknowledge your dissatisfaction and quench the thirst for adventure.

'Follow your bliss and the universe will open doors where there were only walls,' Campbell wrote. That's what the journey encompasses. To accept the quest for more vitality and joy. To let life flow towards you and through you. To discover new doors.

As a writer, you take the call to adventure every time you sit down to write. You escape the world you know to venture into the glorious yet gut-wrenching universe of your fantastical words for as long as you can.

Then because of this, when you do venture back into the real world of domesticity, shopping, cooking, washing and tending to other people's needs, you can return with gratitude, contentment and a loving heart. When you've fulfilled your creative and spiritual needs through the written word, anything is possible and everything is so much more pleasurable.

What's your call to adventure, in your real world and your writer's world?

Reflection and Action

Choose a hero's journey from your past life
and write a one-page story on it.

22. A Woman's Quest
On The Heroine's Journey

Now consider this. The hero's journey is a narrative written by a man, for men. It's a monocultural myth that has been so embedded in our patriarchal society that it seems impossible to unravel.

It's in both the factual and fictional stories we've been enculturated with from Captain Cook's call to adventure and arrival in Australia in 1770 to Luke Skywalker's call to adventure in *Star Wars*. The hero (the man) leaves home, ventures into scary unknown worlds (oceans and galaxies) to conquer and slay the dragons of the inner and outer worlds, before eventually returning home victorious and enlightened.

Time and again we're subjected to the Hollywood version of the hero's journey on the big screen. While more and more women are playing the role of the protagonist taking the hero's journey (think *Alice in Wonderland*, *Wonder Woman*, Katniss in *The Hunger Games* and Elsa in *Frozen*), it's still a role played within the masculine narrative. Moviemakers have cottoned on to the secret that a strong female lead makes for a block-buster movie, even though it's a pseudo declaration that equality matters.

In my view it's a half-hearted nod to gender equality and a diversion from the real issue—women are not born for the hero's journey. Campbell's work is worthy of exploration and consideration to see how it has played out in your life. However, there's another narrative I love for women. It's a new story archetype that represents the unique journey of women, one that doesn't compel us to take the journey alone, to slay the dragons and return triumphant.

Maureen Murdock is a Jungian psychotherapist and was a student of Campbell's. She wrote *The Heroine's Journey: A Woman's Quest for Wholeness* in the early 1990s as a counterpoint to the hero's journey after asking Campbell whether the hero's journey applied to women. Here's how he was purported to have responded: 'Women don't need to make the journey. In the whole mythological tradition, the woman is already there. All she has to do is realise that she's the place the hero is trying to get to.' I imagine that would have been all the fuel Murdock needed to write her book.

Murdock believes the heroine's journey defines the healing of the wounding of the feminine within the patriarchal culture and that the destination is the union between the feminine and masculine. She believes Campbell's model does not address the psycho-spiritual journey of women. 'The feminine journey is about going deep down into soul, healing and reclaiming while the masculine journey is up and out, to spirit.'

Murdock proposes a cycle of ten stages that can be switched around or removed as necessary. They exist with three major stages—The Separation: breaking away from feminine ideals and turning towards patriarchal values. Spiritual Death: turning within to reclaim the power and spirit of the sacred feminine. The Union: the fusion of both feminine and masculine values. While giving many lectures on her model, she also uses it to guide many of her patients through their trauma.

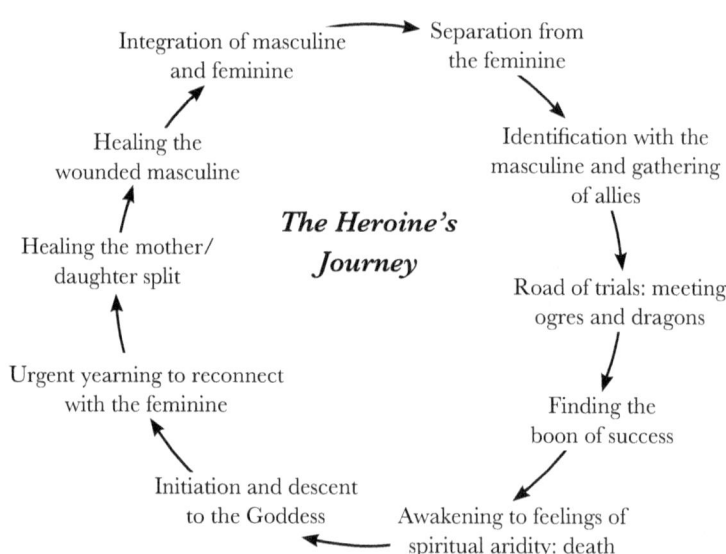

The heroine's journey begins with 'Separation from the feminine' and ends with 'Integration of masculine and feminine.'

Murdock, Maureen, *The Heroine's Journey*, 1990

Separation

1. Separation from the feminine: You begin to distance yourself from anything feminine. You leave the shelter of the archetypal mother to go in search of success and reject the feminine in favour of the masculine.
2. Identification with the masculine: To survive in a male-dominated world you begin to identify with external masculine values, suppressing your inherent feminine traits and rejecting traditional women's activities. You adopt negative masculine traits to be seen and heard.
3. Road of trials: You confront many challenges and obstacles along the way to success as you try to balance your personal and professional life. You must prove to those who think you're not worthy that you can succeed according to male standards and the dominant culture.
4. Finding the boon of success: Having overcome trials you attain success, wealth and adulation. You have it all and feel like a superwoman until you develop feelings of the imposter and recognise this success is illusory.
5. Awakening to feelings of spiritual aridity: Despite your success, you feel empty. You sense there must be something more to life. You start to feel betrayed by 'the system' and by your so-called allies. The inner voice you've been ignoring becomes louder.
6. Initiation and descent to the Goddess: You experience a spiritual crisis, withdrawing from friends and family who are not on the journey. You no longer see the point in struggling for success on old terms. You face your shadow and what is holding you back. You learn to be, instead of just do.
7. Urgent yearning to reconnect with the feminine: You reject the pursuit of outward success and end connections to people and institutions that do not meet your needs for spiritual growth. You turn to creative work and activities that unify mind, heart, body and spirit.
8. Healing the mother/daughter split: You reconnect to your roots and find strength in your her-story. You emerge from the darkness with a deeper sense of self, reclaiming your feminine traits that you once saw as weak. You nurture yourself and are now able to start nurturing and healing others.
9. Healing the wounded masculine: Having reoriented yourself towards your innate feminine essence and reclaimed your place in the world,

you can shed your toxic unhealthy attempts at an adopted but artificial masculinity. You cast aside your unrealistic and illusory concepts of men.

10. Integration of masculine and feminine: You have come full circle. The masculine and feminine traits of your personality are now in union. You are whole and capable of genuine love for all. You recover your true nature.

After graduating from high school in Mount Gambier, in rural South Australia in 1979, I can see that I experienced a major separation from the feminine in favour of the masculine. While most of my female friends went into nursing, teaching or retail jobs, most of my male friends went into banking, accounting and law. While the women took up the work of caring and serving, the men took up the work of money-making, managing and leading.

From memory, most of the women of my day didn't have big dreams. We didn't study feminist icons to whom we could aspire. Germaine Greer. Emmeline Pankhurst. Audre Lorde. Gloria Steinem. Virginia Woolf. (More women to invite to that Deep Dinner along with Maureen Murdock, of course!) We didn't even have feminists in our own town for inspiration (that we knew of anyway), which is sad, because I'm pretty sure at least a few of our female teachers were closet feminists.

Feminism was not even a word in our vocabulary. Instead, we learnt what 'good girls' need to learn to get along in a man's world: typing, home economics, domesticity. We took the path of least resistance to prepare ourselves for what we believed would be our greatest role in life—to become a dutiful woman, wife and mother.

> **In the blink of an eye, the good maths student had become the dutiful employee. I was now working for 'the man' in the man-made world of finance.**

Despite this, I was one of a number of women who fell into the male domain of banking. I remember the job interview vividly. The crusty old bank manager opened his office door, cigarette in hand and looked me up and down from head to toe. I wondered if he was appraising me for a bank job or for the cattle market!? I suppressed the urge to laugh, leave and never return. But I didn't—because I was a 'good girl'. Three days later, I had the job and was wearing a dirty-brown coloured uniform: a very short A-line shift-dress with zero shape to it. It was the ugliest thing I'd ever laid eyes on let alone worn but I had no choice.

In the blink of an eye, the good maths student had become the dutiful employee. I was now working for 'the man' in the man-made world of finance. And so, my accidental twenty-year banking career began. The need for approval from one male boss after another drove my career. I worked hard, achieved my targets and KPIs (key performance indicators) and received rewards for my compliance through promotions and regular salary increases.

While it was satisfying at the time, I didn't question if I'd been born for it. However, I knew deep down that it wasn't really who I was or what I wanted. It just felt like the right thing to do if I was ever going to be 'successful'. It was best to not look back or down, only forward and up, to keep climbing the corporate ladder to who knows where.

> **From memory, most of the women of my day didn't have big dreams. We didn't study feminist icons to whom we could aspire. Germaine Greer. Emmeline Pankhurst. Audre Lorde. Gloria Steinem. Virginia Woolf.**

In 2001, I left the comfort of my family home and my safe banking job, to take the journey. I see that it was more of a hero's journey at the time rather than a heroine's journey. It wasn't until 2011 after our pilgrimage to France that I likely began the heroine's journey. I began to explore and understand how women have been hoodwinked into conforming to the man-made systems of the world.

What about you? What are the stories of your life where you've separated from the feminine to adapt yourself to the world of the masculine? It can be hard to face these truths, to learn that our conditioning was so pervasively strong that we never had the will or the wherewithal to question them and forge our own feminine path.

Time and again, I've found myself back at the first stage of the heroine's journey, acutely aware once more of my conditioning to conform to the man's world. I would either behave like a man or try to please a man, whether it was the man I worked for or the man I was in relationship with. I did it again in my last liaison. I was incapable of accessing my innermost feminine truth, unable to express my womanly desires for fear of appearing needy, expecting too much and being abandoned.

I suspect this is the story for many women. Perhaps our task is to keep returning to the stories in our lives where we've rejected the feminine in favour of the masculine? I should say here that feminine and masculine traits are not gendered. They exist in all of us and in full acknowledgement of the multi-gendered world we live in.

The power of Murdock's model is the call for the continuous healing of our wounded feminine nature so we can integrate the healthy traits of both the feminine and the masculine. The model shows how we can reclaim our deep yearning for the feminine and give life to it through our lives, our communities and our words, while inviting the masculine in to partner with us. To come full circle, to balance the yin and the yang.

Dig out your timeline and identify the pivotal moments in your life where the heroine's journey was at play, the times when you chose the masculine path over the feminine. Perhaps there's a pattern? Or perhaps the journey is appropriate now in light of your current situation? Write these stories. They'll be both revealing and healing in equal measure.

Reflection and Action
Choose a pivotal experience from your life (past or current)
that fits with the heroine's journey narrative
and write a one-page story.

23. Kill the Good Girl
On Many Women's Stories

As each chapter goes by, I feel less inclined to give any more energy to my heartbreak. I think less of him and the dead potential of 'us' and more of me and my own potential—and, of course, you and this book. Each new chapter flushes him out of my system.

And day by day the sorrow subsides. That invisible, oppressive cloak of joylessness that I had about me on the outside, and the sad streak running from head to toe on the inside, has vanished. I'm no longer trapped in a futile holding pattern. I feel freer, happier and more hopeful than I have in a long time.

I'm proving to myself that writing is a powerful elixir for healing grief. I hope that's what your writing is doing for you too. Writing with, and through, the sadness is the only way out. No matter how long it takes. Days. Months. Years. Keep going.

Writing with the rising sun has become my daily prayer and practice. It opens up hope that something new is about to emerge. I have full faith the ensuing chapters of this book will reveal what that is—to me and you.

This morning I finished Patti Smith's book *Just Kids*. It's a must-read for improving your writing skills as Smith shares the inside story of her colourful life as a singer and songwriter and her relationship with the artist, Robert Mapplethorpe, in the sixties.

As I placed the book on top of *The Heroine's Journey* on my bedside table, a random thought occurred. I wondered if Patti and Maureen might be friends in real life, being of the same era. Then I had this surreal vision of them sitting beside me at that Deep Dinner, regaling the whole table with their stories.

This daydream sparked a search for one of my half-written long-forgotten manuscripts, *The Divine Undoing*. It sets out a series of stories tracing the three stages of many women's lives and how we progress from being the 'good girl' (as I referred to it in the opening chapter) to the 'dutiful woman' until we finally choose 'the undoing' of it all, to individuate from the patriarchal paradigm and forge our own path.

> **I'm proving to myself that writing is a powerful elixir for healing grief. I hope that's what your writing is doing for you too.**

I'd written about twenty thousand words, completed a synopsis and pitched a proposal to two publishers who'd both rejected it. It wasn't the rejection that had caused me to stop writing though. It was all the second-guessing myself, the hopping from one manuscript to another, then the lost love and the lost will to write.

At the time of writing it, I'd never heard of the heroine's journey. And now here I was digging back through the twenty or so stories of *The Divine Undoing* attempting to analyse them according to the heroine's journey map.

If you pay attention, you'll find this too. You'll read something new that will spark a memory and prompt you to dig up something old, like a story you wrote aeons ago but never shared. Then voilá! Suddenly your old work finds itself with a new life. No story laying latent but unpublished is wasted. Either they haven't found their time in the sun yet or they've been just the practice you needed.

Here's one of the pieces I'd written for *The Divine Undoing* that's now found it's time in the sun.

I was born a 'good girl'. Both my parents will attest to this.

'You never gave us any trouble. You were always a good girl. Even from grade one, you'd come home from school and sit straight down at the table and do your homework without being asked. You always received good grades. We never had to worry about you,' says my Dad.

'You were quiet and calm. You never bucked the system and always did what you were told. You were very easy to manage', says my Mum. 'As the oldest child, you were very independent quite early and helpful with caring for your siblings.'

They can't recall any instance of me being a 'bad girl' in my early years. While I don't remember the specifics, my parents' recollections ring true for me. I have this overall sense that I was docile, compliant, obedient—almost characterless. I know that I was loved and I had a happy childhood but I was a meek and mild child, a 'good girl' through and through.

The 'good girl' evolves insidiously in our most formative early years. She's gradual, subtle, unconscious and unrecognised but dangerous because she keeps us contained and tamed. A 'good girl' follows in her mother's footsteps, gets the good grades, chooses a career that will make her parents proud, is a dutiful employee and concedes to the will of others.

Later she becomes the 'dutiful woman' who is a heroine on the homefront, the glue of the family and a quiet genius in the kitchen. She plays all the roles she's been groomed for without questioning if something else was meant for her.

What are the behaviours of the 'good girl' turned 'dutiful woman'? Here's a few I've recognised in myself and that my friends have shared with me over the years:

We don't speak up or rock the boat even in situations that are unjust or even harmful.

We always aim to please others even at the expense of our own happiness.

We say a meek yes when we really want to boom a resounding NO.

We avoid conflict at all costs, always trying to smooth things over.

We do what others expect of us, not what we truly want for ourselves.

We accept things without question, particularly from those who assert their authority.

We go along with the majority opinion and often ignore our gut instincts.

We want everyone to like us and care too much what others think.

We can't express our feelings to significant others, particularly the men in our lives who are more convincing or commanding.

We put a lot of energy into hiding our emotions so others won't think we're hysterical or unreasonable.

We apologise all the time when we don't need to.

We give more than we ever receive, which eventually depletes us.

We believe we need a man/partner for our lives to be complete.

We avoid seeking attention or standing out from others.

We constantly compare ourselves to other women.

We don't speak up lest other women criticise us for being too outspoken.

We are overly focused on our body and beauty and want others to admire us for them.

We use silence and tears instead of words and honesty to try to have our needs met.

We expect our partners to know what we want so we don't ask for it or go get it for ourselves.

We put our partner's sexual pleasure before our own.

We step aside and let men, or others we believe are superior, take priority.

We don't take risks because we can't face the shame of incompetence.

That's a long list and I'm sure some resonate for you more than others. Perhaps you have a few more of your own to add. Which ones do you recognise most in yourself? Dig into your 'good girl/dutiful woman' stories. What are they telling you?

Today, I've made friends with my inner 'good girl/ dutiful woman'. I now recognise specific behaviours at play in various situations and notice her. When she appears now, I know how to ask her to step aside and stand up for herself, even to be a 'bad girl/woman' if the situation warrants it. Using this checklist against my romantic relationships was very useful. Try the list against your relationships in life and work. Note the patterns.

'Good girl!' I still hear parents say it to their daughters as a form of praise. It's well-meaning but demeaning. We must stop praising our girls in such a paternalistic way. Instead, we can be more specific with our praise and tell them exactly what they did well and why. And we should do it particularly when they are not 'good girls'. We must do it when they demonstrate a mind of their own, when they colour outside the lines, when they choose un-girly adventures, when they are boisterous, bossy and brave. We must encourage them to develop a character that says, 'I will not be messed with'.

I have compassion for boys and men too. The patriarchal construct girls and women live under does not serve most males either. They're brought up to be 'good boys', to suppress their emotions and 'toughen up'. We are all pawns in the game. We all have much work to do to liberate ourselves and recognise how these behaviours don't serve any of us.

> **No story laying latent but unpublished is wasted. Either they haven't found their time in the sun yet or they've been just the practice you needed.**

If you're a younger woman reading this, you may not believe you are, or have ever been, the 'good girl' or the 'dutiful woman'. In fact, you might reject the theory outright. However, I am sure that somewhere deep down, those two regretful characters cringe. If this idea offends you, don't reject it. Dig into it. It's telling you something. Or think about it in the context of the other women you love. Your grandmother. Your mother. Your sister. Your daughter. Your friend. How does it keep them stuck? How then, does it keep us all stuck?

The 'good girl' is not *who* you are. She is the behaviours you exhibit, and you can change them as quickly or as slowly as your willingness to change allows. When you next interact with people where these behaviours are most likely to appear—with your partner, parents, children or boss—take note and change tack. In the void between stimulus and response, stop, breathe and choose an empowered response instead of the conditioned one. It's that easy—and that hard.

And the next time your mother, sister or friend behaves like the 'good girl' or the 'dutiful woman', find the courage to initiate a kind conversation. Talk about what happened, what it brought up and the pain it triggered for you. This is something I've given full permission to my friends to do with me. I want them to keep me accountable.

We must kill the 'good girl' and the 'dutiful woman' if we are going to create an equal world for women. Through writing and sharing our old stories we can start to shake off the shackles. Dig into your story timeline in search of these stories. Share them with your blood sisters and your chosen sisters and watch the healing begin.

Reflection and Action

Choose a relationship or situation where the
'good girl/dutiful woman' is most at play.
Write its story with a different and empowered ending.

24. Find Your Sister-tribe
On Community

At first, I was lost without him. There were no more weekend escapes to his beach house. No more curling up in the nest we'd created together in my apartment. One minute he was with me, a most important human in my life, the next he was gone. He'd vanished without a trace. I was on my own—again.

Near the end of the last Melbourne lockdown—and the end of our relationship—I paid a rare visit to my local shopping centre. At the top of the escalator, I stepped onto the shiny granite floor and glanced up. A flashing neon sign stopped me dead in my tracks.

'Keep your distance for the wellbeing of our community. Stay 1.5m apart.'

Allowing the people behind me to pass, I found a little corner out of the way and stood there staring at it. Then wrenching my eyes away, I turned my gaze towards my fellow shoppers. If there was any joy in their new-found freedom, there was no evidence of it on their faces. There was an air of fatigue and lifelessness about everyone, as asphyxiating as bushfire smoke.

Tears threatened to erupt as a crushing sadness descended upon me. I squeezed my eyes shut and took a deep breath before resolving to execute my shopping as expeditiously as possible and get away.

At home much later I couldn't shake the sadness. That sign and the whole shopping experience stayed with me all night. I woke up feeling flat and forlorn, wondering what was really bothering me.

I recognised that the wellbeing of humans is heavily dependent on physical as well as emotional touch. Without warm hugs, skin-on-skin contact—and sexual intimacy—our bodies wither and we die. While I appreciated the need to keep apart, the physical distancing of these lockdowns had taken their toll on us.

Next, I turned my attention to one particular word in the sign—community. The shopping centre administrators had got it wrong. The centre felt like a soulless place of individualism and consumerism, not a home for connection, belonging and community. Rebooting the economy was their priority over reconnecting humanity.

> **For millions of people, loneliness *is* the grief.**

I wondered if people really were there to shop or if they were seeking something more? Perhaps an opportunity for a chat, to bond with other humans again? A chance to soothe the loneliness after being home alone for so long?

And then it occurred to me that the suffering in the faces of every human in that centre was a mirror for my own suffering in that moment. I witnessed in them what I'd suppressed in myself. I was forced to admit that I was lonely.

Loneliness. Some believe it's the new pandemic, more harmful to humans than any virus might ever be. Loneliness is the feeling of anxiety, distress or sadness we feel when our relationships fail to meet our expectations. It's a sign they don't meet our deepest need for belonging and connection.

For millions of people, loneliness *is* the grief. And it's not a temporary feeling driven by circumstances like my own, a set of conditions you trust will pass. For so many, it's a chronic, ineradicable sense of disconnection from other humans that's present day after day, year after year with no end in sight.

We may not recognise that our sorrow is due to loneliness. If we do, we're embarrassed or ashamed to admit it and uncertain how to cope. This often results in numbing out through alcohol, drugs, food, shopping and other forms of short-term pain-relief, instead of adopting a healing response.

In the past, my own pain-relief for loneliness after the end of a relationship would be wine and binge-watching TV while texting in the hope he was missing me and that he'd rush straight over. Not so mature—or useful for moving on. This time however, I needed a different response—other than writing of course, which had been lost to me at the time. But what? It turns out that ominous shopping centre sign contained a message for me.

To resolve my loneliness through reconnecting to community.

'We have all known the long loneliness and we have learned that the only solution is love and that love comes with community,' wrote Dorothy Day, the American social activist and anarchist who founded the Catholic Worker Movement.

At Deep Dinners, I often begin with a deep listening exercise. It's a methodology I use to help people connect with each other and unlock their stories. I invite people to split into pairs and ask them to talk for three minutes on this question: 'Aside from your family and friends, what really matters to you, and why?'

The story-teller is asked to keep talking to the end, even if they feel they've said everything. The role of the listener is just that, to listen intently, not ask questions or comment, just be present and then offer feedback without judgement or advice when they have finished. Then they swap over. I urge you to try this exercise at your own Deep Dinner with family and friends. It's the perfect ice-breaker and connector.

When we regather as a group to discuss the exercise, I notice the participants most eager to share are those who have a story about their community. From surf lifesaving to climate-change campaigning to gardening clubs, it's the communitarians who are often the happiest.

It takes a tragedy to strike for people to realise that what matters most for all of us, for the future of humanity and Mother Earth—alongside family and friends—is community. When the pandemic engulfed us and people were forced to work from home, the lonely ones were those who had no community in their streets and suburbs. When the bushfires hit, community came to the rescue. When the floods surged, it was community again.

> **We have all known the long loneliness and we have learned that the only solution is love and that love comes with community.**

Community is where problems are halved and where they are solved together. And it's where all great change begins. Community is found when there is 'common unity', where members share an agreed purpose, where each member can contribute their gift, feel a sense of belonging and make a positive impact. At its core, community expresses creation. It answers the fundamental question Peter Block poses in *Community: The structure of belonging*, 'What can we create together?'

Apart from writing and teaching, my other great passion has always been community-building. I inherited this love from both my parents. The shopping centre experience highlighted I'd lost my connection to community during the pandemic.

I can see now that the sign was a gift, representing an opportunity to start again and consciously create new connections. I made it my mission to reconnect with womenfolk I knew (and some I didn't) who were brave, adventurous, freethinking writers, creators and healers. Women who loved the Yarra Birrarung and river-swimming (my Yarra Yabbies) along with me. Womenfolk (and men) in my suburb and apartment building who were activists for change and passionate about nature and caring for the environment.

I made myself reach out and connect with women who would be good for my soul. It was both a selfish and selfless way to heal my loneliness. That's the two-way healing of a sister-tribe. It can't ever be one way. It's a virtuous circle. What goes around comes around. Every woman matters as we all heal together.

> **It takes a tragedy to strike for people to realise that what matters most for all of us, for the future of humanity and Mother Earth—alongside family and friends—is community.**

Alongside my writers' group and the river, my sister-tribe gave me the fuel I needed to find my way back to the page. Without them I would not have found the courage to write and produce this book. Without a doubt, my wondrous, wild womenfolk are the power behind my words.

When relationships end, when words won't come, when loneliness takes over and your grief is too much to contain on your own, the answer is community. The right community is one where you can be true to yourself, speak your truth and where your big ideas can take root—and where your companions support and applaud your writing efforts.

Of course your loved ones are important, but it's the community of women you belong to and surround yourself with, that hold the secret to your transformation.

If you have a community of brave women behind you, you're lucky. Do not let them go. Invest as much time in them as you do in your family. If you don't have a community, the first work you must do, besides writing, of course, is find one. And if you write not a jot but spend all your time building your sister-tribe, then you are forgiven. Do not stop until you find that circle of courageous and wild women with whom you must belong.

Reflection and Action

Do you have a sister-tribe to belong to?
If so, write a story about them. If not, write a story
about what it would look like and how you will create it.

25. Find Your Sit-spot
On Mother Earth

Johann Hari is the author of *Lost Connections: Uncovering the Real Causes of Depression and the Surprising Solutions.* He posits the theory that depression and anxiety have nine causes. Only two of them are biological and the other seven are to do with the way we live our lives and our unmet human needs. These unmet human needs include lack of meaningful work (purpose), disconnection from other humans (loneliness) and disconnection from the natural world.

'If you're depressed or anxious, you're not crazy or broken—you might just be a human being with unmet human needs,' he shares in his TED talk.

I'm most interested in Hari's theory about disconnection from Mother Nature as a cause of depression. Richard Louv, who first introduced the term Nature-Deficit Disorder in 2005 in his book *Last Child in the Woods: Saving Our children from Nature-Deficit Disorder,* supports the notion.

The book describes the very real cost of our children's alienation from nature. Many adults have the affliction too. So many of us live in a virtual world more connected to our devices and make-believe friends on social media than our real-life friends and our natural world.

I wonder if our virtual-world obsession is also a way to avoid dealing with the reality of the ecological collapse occurring around the globe? If we were to get too close to nature or let ourselves really feel the tragedy of the extinction of animals, the degradation of our reefs, our plastic-polluted oceans and dried up rivers, we may fall into an inescapable pit of grief and hopelessness.

Yet this is exactly what we need to resurrect ourselves. Learning how to become one with nature and simultaneously face the grief of Earth's devastating condition, are essential for finding hope, taking action and writing for change.

Joanna Macy is one of the world's most loved environmental activists' and a deep ecologist. Her book *Active Hope: How to Face the Mess We're in Without Going Crazy* (co-authored by Chris Johnstone) describes finding and deploying our best personal response to the crisis of sustainability unfolding across the planet. It offers tools to help us face our grief, confront the chaos and contribute actively to what they call *The Great Turning*.

I felt grief the last time I snorkelled on the Great Barrier Reef, staring down at the bleached coral and dwindling fish numbers. I felt it during the devastating 2019/20 Victorian bushfires where three billion animals perished. I feel it every time I swim in the Yarra Birrarung and see plastic bottles and polystyrene floating by. I feel it when I see images of all the rivers drying up around the world and imagine it happening here.

I allow myself to feel this grief because I know that without it, my words will fall flat. Then I won't fulfill my purpose to write brave words— or take brave action.

If you are prepared to witness and face the grief beyond your own circumstances—in your own natural backyard and beyond, something shifts in you. Your writing becomes infused with a power you never thought possible.

Grief is no longer a cause of disempowerment but a source of enabled, courageous action. Watch what happens when you feel it and lean into it. When you learn to love grief as much as you love joy, change happens. You can use it to stoke the bonfire of your words—and your life.

To withstand grief and sorrow, we must accept heart break, over and over. 'The heart that breaks open can contain the whole universe. Your heart is that large. Trust it.' says Macy.

When my heart breaks open, whether due to personal or planetary crisis, I immerse myself in the natural world. I recover with, and in, the arms of Mother Earth where I live.

Just as swimming at Deep Rock is a regular practice, so is sitting in my sit-spot in the Koori Revegetation Garden at the confluence of the Yarra Birrarung and Merri Creek. The whole length of the river and the surrounding bush from my home to my sit-spot and swim-spot has become my nature-home, as vital to my wellbeing as my built-home.

I first learned about sit-spots through Claire Dunn's book, *Rewilding the Urban Soul*. A sit-spot is a place you return to daily to sit for at least thirty minutes. The purpose is to observe and absorb the miracle of nature unfolding over time and to learn how to become one with her.

Yet this is exactly what we need to resurrect ourselves. Learning how to become one with nature and simultaneously face the grief of Earth's devastating condition, are essential for finding hope, taking action and writing for change.

'Come forth into the light of things, let nature be your teacher,' said William Wordsworth the English Romantic poet. This is what happens in my sit-spot. I try to practise Dadirri (Aboriginal deep listening) to expand my awareness and welcome nature as my teacher.

My sit-spot is a small, green, wooden bench hidden from the view of passers-by in a grove of young eucalypts on the banks of the river. From this seat I survey the chocolate-brown waters flowing before me. Some days the river flows high and fast, on others, low and gentle.

In this sit-spot I've witnessed two baby white-faced herons grow into young adults. I've seen water dragons skim across the river, scale a tree and morph into chameleon-like statues. I've tuned into the raucous dialect of the rainbow lorikeets chit-chattering away. I've watched the grey-headed flying-foxes swoop down for a drink at dusk during their nightly migration.

It's also a place for dreaming. I've imagined the Wurundjeri Woi Wurrung people gathering here in ceremony more than two centuries ago. I've visualised new projects and next chapters for this book and I've come up with ideas on how to mobilise communities to love and tend this river.

I try to imprint my sit-spot experience in my heart and mind. On my return home, I complete an automatic writing exercise, similar to the morning journal pages but on my laptop. I set a timer for thirty minutes and write about every tiny detail I can recall. I don't pause to think about what I'm writing and I don't stop until the timer goes off. It's the perfect way to find hope and inspire action for the day ahead.

You will find this too. I urge you to find a sit-spot near home, sink into it and write about it. Make it your nature-home, as important to you as your bricks-and-mortar home. Make it a part of your daily life, even if it's just ten minutes a day, then watch what happens to your words and your work.

Through nature journaling, you'll find that bigger questions present themselves. 'What am I being called to change, about my life and the world? What is the small or big change I wish to make—in my own home, street or community? What is the world asking of me?'

As my own boss, I recently gifted myself a four-day work-week. Friday's are my day off for learning, adventuring, immersing myself in nature—or doing absolutely nothing. One drizzly, dreary Friday I chose to snuggle up on my couch to read *Active Hope* from start to finish. I discovered that spending a whole day (and night) reading is just as wonderful as spending a whole day writing.

Macy recommends a powerful activity in her book. She asks readers to assume that Earth could communicate with us. 'If Gaia (the Greek Goddess of Earth, mother of all life) could write a personal letter just to you, what would she write? What would she ask of you?'

An hour or so after beginning this exercise, I looked up to notice that the grey day sky had darkened to a black night sky. My letter had become a ten-page essay, too long to share in full here.

> **When you learn to love grief as much as you love joy, change happens. You can use it to stoke the bonfire of your words—and your life.**

Gaia had urged me to listen ever more deeply to her, to understand that she is hurting, to acknowledge the abuse she's been subjected to and take personal action.

'Along with millions of other humans, you've come to know that our future together is not guaranteed and that just as humans are dependent on me, I am dependent on you. You are as much nature as am I.' she told me.

'You might believe that one little human like you, Carolyn, can make little or no difference. I want you to know that you can—and you must. Swim in me. Sit with me. Write about me. Clean me up. Campaign for me. Learn the calls of the birds, the healing properties of plants, the stories of the Yarra Birrarung River.'

'Learn about Indigenous history, the original custodians of the land and the Wurundjeri Woi Wurrung people who lived here. Keep practising Dadirri. Learn more about indigeneity and how to find a home in me with the Aboriginal people. Know that you belong here too.'

'You have many gifts to share, Carolyn. The next one is in the publishing and sharing of this book with as many women as possible. This book is far from perfect, but it's good enough. Do not let fear of what others may think get in the way. Get it done and get it out. Women need to read it because they want to make an impact with their words and deeds too.'

'Don't devote any more energy to your past lover. He's nothing compared to what's waiting for you. Trust your future and trust me. I know what's best for you. Get on with dating. Open your heart again. Be brave.'

And Gaia's final sentence . . .

'In the end, Carolyn, all we have is love. Love is the only response. Love is the true quest. Keep loving.'

Note: We now have two more women to invite to that Deep Dinner: Joanna Macy and Claire Dunn. I also wonder if Gaia might somehow be present?

Reflection and Action
Write your own letter from Gaia to yourself
then share it with a friend or your writers' group.

26. The Finish Line
On Facing Fear

As I've already shared, for three long years the manuscript for *Unstuck in Provence* remained untouched and unpublished. I'd not shared the manuscript with a soul, not even my sisters or Billy. Every few months I'd dig it up from my computer files and wistfully read parts of it only to return it from whence it came. I was like an old dog returning to a buried bone for a nostalgic gnaw before re-internment.

Many times I hovered on the brink of publication only to find myself caught up in some other project or distraction. The truth was that I lacked the courage to put my life (and Billy's) up for scrutiny. It was an intimate, tell-all book and I wasn't sure either of us was ready to have our private lives made public.

Fear had prevented me from finishing.

Fear gripped me in its jaws. Fear of my son's reaction and possible rejection. Concern over a potential lawsuit from my ex-lover and/or my ex-husband. Anxiety at my mother's and father's reaction. Nervousness over what my sisters and girlfriends would think. Dread that readers and critics would judge my book as self-indulgent and amateur. Worry it would be seen as a cheap *Eat Pray Love* knock-off. Concern that it would damage my business reputation. Doubt that I would ever live up to that commitment statement I'd penned in France in a moment of bravado and self-confidence. So much fear.

I read Brené Brown's, *Daring Greatly* at the time. She made *The Man in the Arena* speech by Theodore Roosevelt modern again with her re-interpretation.

'It is not the critic who counts; not the man who points out how the strong man stumbles, or where the doer of deeds could have done them better. The credit belongs to the man who is actually in the arena, whose face is marred by dust and sweat and blood; who strives valiantly; who errs, who comes short again and again, because there is no effort without error and shortcoming; but who does actually strive to do the deeds; who knows great enthusiasms, the great devotions; who spends himself in a worthy cause; who at the best knows in the end the triumph of high achievement, and who at the worst, if he fails, at least fails while daring greatly, so that his place shall never be with those cold and timid souls who neither know victory nor defeat.'

I wasn't in the arena. I wasn't daring greatly. I was a timid and fearful soul languishing on the side-lines. In the end the fear that this book would remain unpublished outweighed all my other anxieties. *The Man in the Arena* became the kick up the proverbial I needed to act.

If I couldn't *be* the best, I would at least *do* my best and finish what I'd begun.

One Sunday morning, I printed out the manuscript and when the moment was right, told Billy that I was ready to publish it. 'Would you please read it and share your thoughts on it with me? I'd be happy to eliminate or change anything you're not comfortable with,' I offered. 'Sure,' he responded, showing not a modicum of interest as I handed him the string-bound pages.

For three weeks I resisted the temptation to press him for his response. I had no idea if he'd even given it any thought let alone his undivided attention. For all I knew, he'd just tossed it in his cupboard unread. He was sixteen years old by then, so *World of Warcraft*, socialising and getting through school were his main concerns. He had long forgotten our French sojourn.

Then one day he walked into my bedroom and tossed the manuscript on my bed. 'Mum, it's brilliant. I've written my comments in pen and edited some bits I didn't like. You can't write things like OMG—only kids use those expressions. I reckon lots of mums will be inspired by your story. You should publish it.' And with that he turned on his heel and retreated to his room. No angst. No complaints. No questions.

Fear had prevented me from finishing.

I laughed aloud with relief. A single moment of approval from my son released all those pent-up fears. It was the key to unlocking the magic door and powering on to publication. Billy's approval gave me the courage to share the manuscript with my ex-husband. And my ex-lover?

I changed his name and made him unidentifiable. In doing so, I had no need to share it with him.

So often, the fear of what might happen, or what other people might think, holds us back from going that last mile. We choose to stay small, avoid risks and remain anonymous instead of taking a leap and sharing our work.

> If I couldn't be the best, I would at least do my best and finish what I'd begun.

If your desire is to share your words with the world, at some point you will need to face your fears. And to face your demons, you must first name them.

Fear your writing is rubbish.

Fear someone will call your work a knock-off of someone else's words.

Fear that it's not original.

Fear you've written something that could end up in a legal battle.

Fear there'll be mistakes in it. (I've never read a book that hasn't had a mistake.)

Fear that readers and critics will give it a scathing review.

Fear of hateful and hurtful comments from trolls. (Those always on the side-line, never in the arena.)

Fear no one will buy it.

Fear it will not be a best-seller. (Whatever that is.)

Fear it will be a huge, embarrassing flop, something of which you'll die of shame.

Fear your best friends, family and all the people you really love, will hate it. (Don't worry, most won't even read it.)

Name your fear here ...

Once you've named the fears, you can then acknowledge them and thank them for showing up. Rather than shuffling them offstage, I recommend giving them attention and working through them. Get to know your enemies. You might even make friends with them. Journal your way through them. Find a way to manage them so they won't debilitate you.

Here's a way I relieve my fears these days. Once you've named your fears, work through each one as follows:

My fear is ...

The worst that can happen if this fear comes to fruition is ...

The best that can happen if this fear is false is ...

Then keep writing on the fear. Over time it will dissipate and you'll be liberated.

Here's an example for *Unstuck in Provence*:

My fear is that my ex-husband (Billy's father) will be angry, ask me not to publish it and take legal action. The worst that can happen is that we will end up in court. The best that can happen is that he will be happy for me to publish it and congratulate me.

Two agonising weeks after emailing him the manuscript, he came back with a very generous response saying, 'thank you for being so sensitive and kind. I am happy for you to publish it and good luck with it'. He stopped short of coming to the book launch but he did send me his well wishes. This is what can happen when you name and face your fears. Anything at all can happen. And it's rarely as bad as we might expect.

'When I look back on all these worries, I remember the story of the old man who said on his deathbed that he had had a lot of trouble in his life, most of which had never happened,' wrote Winston S. Churchill.

> **Writing is a most fear-inducing vocation. It brings up those two diametrically opposed feelings of fear and love in equal measure every day.**

After you've written your way through each fear, you must act and take one immediate bold step forward. Email your work (even if only half complete) to someone you trust. Call a successful published friend and ask advice on how to publish it. Turn your story into a PDF and share it with five friends. Do anything to get over your fear and get it out.

Writing is a most fear-inducing vocation. It brings up those two diametrically opposed feelings of fear and love in equal measure every day. Yet the tension between these two emotions results in great writing. The fears are there to serve you; they test your commitment to your craft.

I'm intrigued as to why we writers are so anxious and full of fear when it comes to our creative writing endeavours. We don't seem to have the same fears about other major life pursuits: partnering, parenting or our paid professions, even though time and again we fall short in these roles. Somehow, when it comes to writing (or other creative endeavours), we can't accept that we're not perfect or that we might fail so we either don't start or we give up too soon and never get to the finish line.

If you don't publish, you'll fail anyway. If you do publish you have a fifty-fifty chance of failure or success. And what is failure versus success anyway? They are both subjective notions. In my view, if your work heals you and helps just one other person, that's success.

Feel the Fear and Do It Anyway is the title of the huge best seller by US psychologist and author, Susan Jeffers. Is there really any other way?

Reflection and Action

What are the three top fears you face when it
comes to writing and sharing your work?
Write your way through them.

27. A Second Life
On Editing

Note: The following chapters are devoted to the subjects of editing, publishing and marketing a book. No matter your writing project, however, you'll find these practices helpful as you step closer towards sharing your words with the world.

How's your writing coming along? Have you been keeping at it? Are you right beside me working on your craft?

I have exactly twenty days to achieve my goal. Seven chapters and an epilogue—about twelve thousand words till I type The End. What's your goal? Will you make it? I'm right here cheering you on. Can you feel it?

About now you should put up your 'Do Not Disturb' sign, clear the diary of non-essential activities and eliminate all distractions. You must do whatever it takes to meet your lifeline (as opposed to deadline). All that matters is that you complete your first draft.

Perhaps, as you near your lifeline, you're wondering what will happen the day after you type those inimitable words The End. It's right to start thinking about this, to devote a little time to plan what's next. It will give you the impetus you need to keep going. And it will ensure your words don't end up in some dark, forgotten file.

Side note: Have you been saving and backing up as you go? On your cloud storage, on your laptop, as a printed version and emailed to a friend or two? Do them all.

I'll never forget the heart-breaking conversation I had with a fellow author while I was in France. She'd just completed her magnum opus and had been saving it diligently to her laptop. In Paris, en route to her husband's office to print it out, she'd become gridlocked in traffic. Before she knew what had happened, a hooded thief appeared from nowhere, yanked open the back door of her Citroën and snatched the laptop. Two years of painstaking labour and love—gone in seconds. It makes me weep to think of it. Don't let this happen to you.

Once you get to the end of your first draft, you'll need a circuit breaker, something to take you away from your words for a while to celebrate your achievement. I have a long weekend planned post typing The End. An immersive nature experience: camping, swimming and bushwalking with friends at one of Victoria's gorgeous waterholes. It will be the beginning of a month-long break from writing.

After exactly a month, I'll get to work on the second draft. I've accepted this book will need reordering and a whole lot of rewriting. I've written the bare bones of it but they still need the flesh.

> **Have you been saving and backing up as you go? On your cloud storage, on your laptop, as a printed version and emailed to a friend or two? Do them all.**

While your first draft is a good start, it's just a pile of words strung together. It's the beginnings of *a* book, but it is not *the* book you had hoped to write—yet. You might not want to hear those words at this juncture but best you know now so you can plan for it.

With the first draft, you have the core of your book. You know where you're going. You know all the answers to *why, what, who* and *how*. You know the plot, you've developed the characters, you have the flow. You've said a lot of words straight but perhaps not that great yet.

Think of it as though you're building a new house. You've designed it, set the foundations, erected the walls and fitted a roof. You have enough to protect you from the elements but you can't live in it. That's where you stand with the first draft. You have an uninhabitable house with a lovely vision for its completion.

The second draft adds those aspects that make your house almost liveable. The flooring. The internal walls. The appliances. The open fireplace. The bath. The blinds. You get the picture. But it's the third and (perhaps) final edit that turns your house into a home. This is where you and/or your editor add the comfy sofa, the plants, the artwork and the soul. You light that open fire, uncork the Veuve Clicquot and drink a toast with your family and friends. You turn your words into a book your reader can't put down.

You'll need to make as much time for the second draft as you did your first. If you want a brilliant book, you're going to have to do a serious edit or rewrite. You can hand this off to an editor or you can do it yourself.

It will depend on how complete you believe your work is and whether you have a deal with a publishing house or are paying an independent company to manage the whole process from editing to printing. Either way, I'm an advocate for doing the second draft yourself.

Before you begin your next draft, I recommend finding two or three readers from your ideal audience who'd be willing to read it and offer feedback. Not close friends or family members but people who you think are likely to buy your book. They should be avid readers of other books in your genre and willing to provide constructive feedback. Be clear about the feedback you want. They are not there to correct your grammar or proof-read your spelling. Their purpose is to offer ways to make your manuscript more compelling.

My editor Roger McDonald recommends asking your test readers these questions:

What is this book about?
How could it more effectively make its point?
How is it different to other books of its kind or genre?
What did you like about the book?
What did you dislike or disagree with?
How does the personality of the author come through?
How could this book influence or change the lives of readers?

From past experience, it can be daunting when you first receive the feedback. You should be thankful for it and accept it with gratitude. Acknowledge it. Consider it. Then when you're ready, discern and decide what feedback you'll incorporate in the next draft and what you'll leave behind. Remember, it's your book. And try your best not to take any of the not-so-good feedback personally. You must learn to develop a hide as thick as a horse.

That's where you stand with the first draft. You have an uninhabitable house with a lovely vision for its completion.

After the first-readers' feedback I'll also do a quicker third edit then hand it off to Roger for the final edit before production and its release to the world. It's a process.

The hardest part of authorship is getting over the hump from the end of the first draft manuscript to publishing. My advice is to stick with it, step by step.

Small Business Big Brand taught me the hard way about editing and

> **The hardest part of authorship is getting over the hump from the end of the first draft manuscript to publishing. My advice is to stick with it, step by step.**

self-publishing. After completing the first draft, I proudly printed it out and handed over the pages to my friend, Nikki Cripps, a journalist, copywriter and editor.

'Can you please give it a read, tell me what you think and help me get it published by 1 January?' I asked. This was just three months away and I was convinced it was ready for publication. In all earnestness and with utter naivety, I believed my words were ready just as they were. I had no idea about second drafts, the different levels of editing or much else. To top it off, I'd already booked the venue and organised a guest list for the book launch in February. There was no time to waste.

For a few weeks I was on tenterhooks waiting for Nikki's verdict. I resisted calling her to check on progress. Finally, she got back to me. 'I think it's pretty good but it needs quite a bit of work.' What!? I hadn't counted on this. I was at a loss as to what to do. In an instant, I lost all faith in my words so I handed it back to Nikki to have her way with the manuscript pronto, fortunately at a mates-rates price.

While I was waiting for Nikki, I had my graphic artist prepare the cover design and some initial internal sketches and layouts. Midway through December, Nikki handed me back a much-improved manuscript. She'd given it a second life. It seemed like it was all coming together. Now I could finally get this book printed and out in the world.

Or could I?

Soon after, my dear friend, Vesna Maletic, visited from Adelaide. On the night she arrived, she offered to give the manuscript a final read before sending it to the designer. Vesna, being the thorough woman she is, suggested it needed quite a few small but worthy amendments which resulted in us spending an entire night immersed in one final proof-read over a whole tin of shortbread biscuits and endless cups of tea. All these years later, we still laugh about that 'holiday' she was meant to have with me.

At last I could send it to the designer for layout and preparation of the files for printing. Little did I know how long it would take to proof-check every single page to make sure it was laid out just right before printing. With just two weeks until the launch date, I hit the print button. But there was no guarantee from the printer that my first copies would be ready in time. I remember thinking that writing the actual book was a doddle compared to the editing, production and publishing process.

The day before the launch, two hundred copies of *Small Business Big Brand*, my first ever book, arrived on my home-office doorstep. The books were hand-delivered by the printer himself with a grin from ear to ear. I might have even kissed him.

All these wonderful people have in some way, big or small, contributed to the evolution of my writer's life. From the woman who owned that tiny cabin where I first began my book-writing adventures to the printer and all the hundreds of people since who've played a part. And, of course, every dear reader who has bought the book. Writing and publishing is the ultimate heroine's journey and it's only possible with other beautiful souls by your side.

You may even love writing your second draft manuscript as much the first. Mostly because you get to write your straight words better and there's a delicious thrill in turning lifeless sentences into life-giving lessons. It's also an opportunity to embed the words and wisdom they contain in your psyche—and that's where another layer of healing happens.

Somehow, as you give your manuscript a second life, the work becomes you—and you become the work. It refuels your courage and conviction to keep writing, no matter what.

Reflection and Action
Take a piece of your writing and give it a second
life (edit) and note the difference.

28. On the Shelf
On Publishing

'Write drunk. Edit sober.' The quote is often misattributed to Ernest Hemingway who rarely, if ever, wrote under the influence of any substance. No matter. It gave me the permission I needed to get through the writing of my second book *Marketing Your Small Business for Dummies*. While I wasn't falling-down drunk, the two big bold glasses of cabernet each night kept me writing. And they gave me the tone of voice perfect for the *Dummies* style.

The *Dummies* book came about because the publishers at Wiley had their hands on *Small Business Big Brand*. When they approached me to write it, I was undecided. I knew it would build the *Dummies* brand rather than my own. I had to weigh up the pros and cons. It required quite a degree of work on my part before they'd even offer a contract.

The lure of a healthy advance and the opportunity to experience working with a substantial publishing house won me over. Before signing the deal, I had to submit a proposed Table of Contents, provide a sentence outlining the point of each chapter and write one complete chapter for assessment. This gave me an insight into the process and time to establish trust in my agent so I was confident in accepting the contract.

The turn-around time was tight and I ended up writing day and night, seven days a week for six weeks to finish the first draft manuscript. I devoted myself to meeting that lifeline and those two glasses of cabernet each night got me through.

Handing over the manuscript to Wiley's was a huge relief. Now it was all out of my hands. The second and third edits, legal signoffs, indexing, layouts, images, design, back cover blurb, distribution, marketing and PR—Wiley would handle it all. Note: Publishers today expect their authors to market and sell their own book. As this was a *Dummies* branded book, they had no expectation of me to do this at the time.

That's the advantage of working with a commercial publisher. They take away some of the hard labour of getting your book out into the world. They have a process. The good ones know exactly what they're doing. They deal with the painful parts most writers are not equipped to manage, leaving you free to get on with your next work. And unlike self-publishing, there is no further expense for you. And the biggest benefit? Distribution. They can get your book into bookshops and places denied you as a self-published author.

On the downside, the publishing house owns your words. The book becomes their copyright, not yours. And the royalties from your book will most definitely not be enough to put food on the table, unless of course you've written a Booker Prize winner.

Also, they will publish the book according to their schedule and time-frames, not yours. If your book is ready for the production line and you must get it to market urgently, a publishing house probably won't come to the party. And finally, these days they'll expect you to provide a thorough marketing plan, your own brand, database and social media presence and an ability to get the cash registers ringing. In the many pitches I've made to publishers, my ability to market my own book was just as important as the quality of my content.

> **Most authors will tell you that each book they write leads to the next.**

We launched *Dummies* in June 2010 at a small gathering hosted by a generous client. Within weeks I'd largely forgotten it, confidently leaving Wiley's to do the marketing grunt work. Completing the book confirmed the uncomfortable realisation that while I loved writing, I'd lost my passion for old-school marketing. Besides, I was planning my next adventure with Melbourne and France just months away.

Most authors will tell you that each book they write leads to the next. *Small Business Big Brand* led to the invitation to write the *Dummies* book which led to another commission from Wiley's to write *Conscious Marketing* on my return from France. *Conscious Marketing* was my last-ditch attempt at making marketing a force for good in the world with a purpose beyond profit as its central tenet. This led me to research the subject of purpose as the driver for humans, business and to writing *The Purpose Project*.

Unstuck in Provence was left of field from the others. It was the turning point where I realised I could write whatever was in my heart, not what my head said I must write for business purposes. It became a catalyst for this book, just as this book begins to form the catalyst for the next one already giving me disturbed nights.

One way to propel yourself through the process from finished manuscript to published book is to have your next writing project in mind. It makes you want to finish your current book fast and it helps release the severe attachment you might have to it.

All these years later, the *Dummies* book is still in publication and I'm forever grateful for the opportunity Wiley's gave me. I learnt to navigate the tricky world of contracts and agreements, writing to a structure, style, word-count and delivering to agreed timeframes. It also, paradoxically, gave me the confidence to step into the world of self-publishing. I learnt the process of publishing and as a marketer with project management experience, I became confident in self-publishing.

Since *Dummies*, the publishing world has been flipped on its head. It's not so easy to secure an advance from a traditional publishing house. I've even heard that authors are now starting to pay publishing houses to publish their book.

Most authors in my network own a small business and publish books in their specific field as a way to share their knowledge and secure new clients. Many now choose self-publishing and working with reputable small businesses who do everything from coaching you to write your book to managing the entire self-publishing process. These businesses do everything the big publishing houses would do, and more.

They manage the process from the first edit right through to publishing your book, your launch and the management of marketing and PR. If you don't think you'll be able to secure a publishing deal, I'd recommend looking into this. While it costs anything from five thousand to twenty thousand dollars, it's a worthwhile investment if you can afford it. If you can't, you can still take a fully DIY approach and learn the tricks of the trade yourself using publishing platforms with next to no fees. Or you can just save your book as a PDF and email it to people or produce it as a series of weekly blogs.

> **One way to propel yourself through the process from finished manuscript to published book is to have your next writing project in mind. It makes you want to finish your current book fast and it helps release the severe attachment you might have to it.**

You now have so many options to get your words out into the world. When necessity is the mother of invention, you'll find a way.

I self-published *The Purpose Project* in 2017 on a platform called Ingram Spark (which many author friends use too). It's a print-on-demand service which means a reader in any country can order just one copy through any of thousands of retail platforms from Amazon to Booktopia and have it delivered to their door without you having to lift a finger. It also provides the platform for the book's distribution in digital formats from Kindle to iBooks.

I do not profess to be a publishing expert. There are many reliable experts and texts on how to choose the best pathway to publishing, including how to work with an agent who can represent you to publishing houses. I recommend joining a reputable organisation like the Australian Society of Authors, researching all the options, attending educational events and courses, learning from others and sinking yourself into the world of publishing. It's a minefield but it's worth navigating.

So how will I publish *Brave Women Write*?

I remain open to the process. All I know is that, by hook or by crook, I will launch and publish it by the end of 2022.

While the final edit is in my editor, Roger's, hands, I'll dig into my list of publishing contacts that I've accumulated over the years. I'll send an email to a few asking if they're interested in me submitting a proposal and chapter of the book. While I'm waiting for a response, I'll push ahead with self-publishing. I'm confident I can project manage it with a few independent professionals such as Roger, a designer and a web-developer.

To get your book published, open yourself to all possibilities. Don't go in with a narrow idea of how it must get to market. You can have all the control in the world over the writing but publishing is the difficult and sometimes disappointing sequel. If you want a publishing house to pick it up, you'll have much work to do. It may be better to self-publish. On a positive note, even if you do take the plunge to self-publish in the beginning, that doesn't preclude a publishing house picking it up at a later stage.

> **Whether you have a *Harry Potter* on your hands or not, you must believe your story matters and that it deserves to be read.**

A dozen publishers turned down JK Rowling before Bloomsbury picked up the *Harry Potter* series. I'll bet the publishers who wrote those rejection letters are still kicking themselves.

Whether you have a *Harry Potter* on your hands or not, you must believe your story matters and that it deserves to be read. Keep writing. Don't stop. Get to the end. Put your mind to publishing matters later.

Reflection and Action

Imagine you have three minutes to pitch your book to a publisher. Write your pitch script.

29. Making Waves
On Launching and Marketing

Imagine your book is now with an editor in its final stages. You now have time to breathe and take a well-earned rest for a while, right? Wrong. This is the very time you must start marketing it. Assuming you're self-publishing your book, now is the time to create a plan and let potential readers know your book will soon appear.

Here are a few things I've learned on over the years on producing, launching and marketing my books.

1. Naming and designing your book.
Your marketing starts with the title, subtitle and cover design of your book. It's what grabs people's attention and makes them pick up and buy your book. It doesn't guarantee that people will read it though. What's on the inside ultimately gets them from front cover to the last page.

When the right person buys it, reads it and loves it, they'll offer reviews and recommend it to their friends. That's what you're aiming to do with your book, to get people to read the book and share it.

When it comes to titles, don't make the mistake of settling on one title before, or as you write, your first draft. It's like deciding on your baby's name before they're born. When your sweet little cherub arrives, the name may not feel right at all. They're born for a different name. Experienced authors often only consider the title after they complete the second or even third draft. They believe that the book creates the title, not the other way round.

Choosing a title is not so simple. Start by researching the list of titles in your genre. Pick out the ones you love most. You'll now know what you can't use but also find inspiration to come up with something just as creative.

Here are some ideas for name generation.

Use an online book title generator (yes, they exist.)

Write down the problem your book solves in one sentence to inspire the subtitle.

Conduct a social media poll with three to five potential options.

Ask your first readers and editor to summarise your book in one sentence and use their words to generate a title.

If you have a publisher on board, work with them to determine the best title. They should have all the intelligence on what sells in your genre.

Use a famous quote to inspire your title, or even a sentence of your own book.

When it comes to book cover design, look to your library or bookshelf for inspiration and go online to see what other covers you love. If you can afford it, pay a professional cover designer, someone who is experienced and knows your genre. I've learnt that cover design is a special art.

In my view, editing and book cover designers are the two most important investments for self-publishers. Your cover design and title have the power to make or break your book—along with your words, of course. Choose wisely.

2. Launching your book.

Your marketing should start well before the launch date—the date your book is available for purchase and can reach the hands of happy readers. As I've done for each of my books, I'll host a launch function with family, friends, clients and business associates to mark the occasion.

> **Marketing and selling can be so much fun but they require ingenuity, personality and even a little outlandishness.**

With *The Purpose Project,* which I self-published, I hosted a cocktail party in a private room at a pub in Melbourne's trendy Fitzroy. Over one hundred guests purchased a ticket and came to help me celebrate. There was a glass of bubbly on arrival and canapés for everyone. Financially it was a break-even event and I surprised guests with two signed copies of the book, one for themselves and one to pass onto a friend as part of a 'pay it forward' campaign.

As soon as this manuscript goes to Roger for editing and I have the book cover design, I'll begin marketing it online. My web developer will build a one-page website where I'll offer pre-sales and sell tickets to the launch event. I'll publish weekly blogs with excerpts from the book, send newsletters to my mailing list and share snippets of the book on my social media.

No matter how you launch your book, whether at a small family gathering or a large online launch event, it's important to mark your achievement in a way that's meaningful to you. Please don't let this momentous occasion go by uncelebrated.

3. Marketing your book.

The first month after your launch is the most crucial time for marketing and sales. You'll need to devote all your time and energy to having as many of your books as possible in the hands of readers and to seek as many book reviews (on Amazon and other platforms) as possible. They'll become your first influencers and advocates.

> **But perhaps the ultimate marketing advice I can offer is to ensure you have the right mind-set. You must wholeheartedly believe in your book.**

With *The Purpose Project,* I made it my mission to have one thousand books in the hands of readers within a month. I made the goal public and I posted a short video each day sharing my progress. As each day went by, my followers grew more invested in helping me achieve my goal. I'd created a little movement and ended up achieving my target: I gave away three hundred books to influencers and sold more than seven hundred.

After the first month, take a breath, review your progress then make a plan for the next ninety days. And then the next ninety days and so on. You must never stop marketing your book if you want to give it the best chance of a long shelf-life.

Two months after the launch of *The Purpose Project*, I took to the road on a ten-week book tour to ten cities across Australia and the United States where I hosted Deep Dinners, met with influencers and spoke at events, including an address to Professor William Damon and the faculty at the Centre on Adolescence at Stanford University.

My goal was to make one hundred thousand impacts through blogs, podcasts, video posts, social media, dinners, speaking engagements and book sales. In the end, however, I made only forty thousand impacts and another one thousand book sales. For a while after I got home, I rolled around like a petulant child in the dirt of disappointment at the numbers. But in time, I put on my big-girl pants and recognised it was a decent effort.

I've yet to decide what my marketing and sales plan will be in 2023 and beyond for this book. I'm just focusing on the immediate goal of publishing then selling in time for Christmas.

The greatest marketing tool for your book is word-of-mouth. There's nothing more powerful than writing a book that hits your ideal reader in the heart and that's so compelling they tell everyone about it. So, gather a tribe of your first followers, build a relationship with them and let them know you appreciate their support. Reward them for their loyalty. Then watch your words make waves.

The day will come when you must turn your attention to the world beyond your comfortable writing hidey-hole. You'll need to have a plan to get your book into the hands of readers. When that day comes, you must tap into the same exquisite creative depths you found in the process of writing your book. Marketing and selling can be so much fun but they require ingenuity, personality and even a little outlandishness. An open, playful, anything-is-possible approach is the way to cut through.

But perhaps the ultimate marketing advice I can offer is to ensure you have the right mind-set. You must wholeheartedly believe in your book. You must love it like you would your only child. You must know the world needs your words, that you are offering a gift, a way to be of service, a solution to transform your readers' lives. When you know this, then all will be well with your book and it will have a happy, healthy life.

Reflection and Action

Write a vision for your book launch.
Where will it be, what will happen and who will be there?

30. Money, Money, Money
On Making a Living

Can you make money from your book? Yes. No. Maybe. Don't count on it.

The most marvellous book in the world won't earn a cent without a marketing machine behind it. And the most abominable book on the planet can make millions if it finds an untapped market and has the backing of an intensive, focused marketing and advertising plan.

Take *Fifty Shades of Grey*. Opinions vary widely. Some think it's brilliant. Some think it's appalling. My mother always said, 'If you can't say something nice, don't say anything at all.' I'm saying nothing. According to the *Guardian*, it's number five on the top one hundred best-selling books of all time after a few of the *Harry Potter* titles and the *Da Vinci Code*. The book has sold nearly four million copies. You work it out.

Fifty Shades of Grey tapped into an unmet need of women everywhere. It proved that we hunger for sexual liberation. It had a clear cause and it began some sort of movement.

However, books sold and money made, are not the most important measure of your book's success. I believe they're secondary to the value you gain from the experience and the time spent thinking, creating and producing those precious, life-affirming words. The pure joy you've experienced. The healing you've found. The cause you've advanced. The readers you've influenced by your words. The new vocation or career it might lead to. The fact that you've fulfilled your purpose beyond all your main roles in life—worker, mother, partner, carer, homemaker. This is what you must value.

Writing a book is a life-changing experience. It's not one that must always have a huge financial return-on-investment.

The likelihood you'll make substantial money from book sales is close to zero considering the number of books published globally. Here are some sobering facts. Research suggests that the average self-published book will sell only about two hundred and fifty copies. By comparison, the average book published by a traditional publishing house will sell about three thousand. Ten thousand book sales is considered an excellent result.

With *The Purpose Project*, I've sold over ten thousand books so far and made more than fifteen thousand dollars in profit. That does not account for the website and book tour costs and the time spent blogging, on social media, doing podcast interviews and the like. But I'm still proud of that effort when so many authors I know make a loss on their books.

> **Writing a book is a life-changing experience. It's not one that must always have a huge financial return-on-investment.**

The greatest value of the book, though, has been that it has positioned me as an expert in purpose and story-telling. It's led to teaching and consulting work and enabled me to make an independent living doing what I love.

I hope that those who read and enjoyed my last books will be inclined to purchase *Brave Women Write*. The more books you write, the more people trust your work and the more they'll read you and recommend you. Past book sales can beget new book sales.

Before setting sales expectations, it's worth reconsidering why you decided to write the book in the first place. What was your purpose? Go back to that *Chapter 17 Why? What? Who?* and revisit your thirty-three reasons why.

Was it to leverage your expertise and build credibility to secure new clients? Was it to record your life-story or your family history to preserve for future generations? Was it because you had a very specific story to tell and you wanted to experience how it feels to accomplish a goal you've always wished to achieve? Or was it to advance a cause, share your knowledge on your subject of passion or an item to tick off your bucket-list?

Or was it to write a best-seller that would make you millions? I'm willing to bet you didn't list that as one of those thirty-three reasons why, and if it was, it was way down the list. It's not everyone's dream to achieve fame and fortune or even enough to make a living from writing. Writing and publishing a book is a huge accomplishment in itself, something to be celebrated and proud of.

Sometimes, even if your book is brilliant, it might not sell well due to poor (or no) marketing. Or your book might not hit the mark. It just might be a flop. Keep marketing it and get writing again. Or stop marketing it and start writing better.

An old saying suggests, 'the best way to get over someone is to get under someone else'. It's the same with books, 'the best way to get over your book flopping is to start writing the next book.'

If you want to turn your words into bread and butter, don't quit your day job to write until your bank statement shows writing has become your day job.

I work in the world of small business owners and entrepreneurs who are knowledge workers, thought leaders or specialists in their field. They're usually highly educated, qualified and experienced and are dedicated to leading movements in their subject matter of expertise: positive psychology, education, mental health, innovation, climate-change, anthropology, gender equality and more.

Of these people, ninety-nine percent are not household names, yet they make a healthy living from leveraging their work. They've written books, not because it's their purpose in life, but to generate business. They give more away as expensive business cards than they sell. They write their books to prove and reinforce their expertise and credibility and to open the doors (and wallets) of potential clients.

Experts write books as a pathway to selling programmes, speaking engagements, coaching, consulting, mentoring, teaching, advising, facilitating, project managing, designing, accounting, lawyering, drafting, editing, copywriting, producing, content-managing, campaigning and even writing for other clients.

Combine your book with a specific service offering, programme or course for a niche audience and you might just be able to build a healthy business from it. Many programmes can teach you how to do this. I've dabbled in a good few but mostly trusted my own gut.

The Purpose Project led to developing an online course which, to be honest, has not been a best-seller. I learned so many lessons there but it has also led to

> **If you want to turn your words into bread and butter, don't quit your day job to write until your bank statement shows writing has become your day job.**

sales of my *Talk on Purpose* course, now delivered in schools and businesses where it is doing well. Writing and teaching are my twin passions. I've had good years and not-so-good years financially. That's the risk of being in business. Yet I'm still Zooming and standing and delivering with more than enough time for writing. I wouldn't have it any other way.

I'm not yet sure what this book will lead to. Perhaps writers' workshops for women? Or speaking gigs? Or mother and daughter writing circles? You tell me. I remain open to the possibilities. Write. Teach. Write. Teach. Write. Teach. That's my lot in life till the day I depart. And I still wouldn't have it any other way.

If you're keen to make a living from your writing, here are some ideas to explore.

Review the purpose for writing the book. Do you need to make money from it? Find out what other authors in your genre are doing and how they're making a living. Attend networking events and meetup groups where others are making a living from their words. Consider one of the many reputable courses and programmes that teach you how to make a living from your book.

Create a programme/course offer based on the contents of your book and test it with a group of people over a Deep Dinner. In my experience, a book gives people enough confidence to buy your services, even if you haven't built the course yet. It's almost a case of engineering the plane while you're flying it. If you sell the learning intention and outcomes you can then be agile building it. And you can even invite your clients to help you co-create your programme as you teach it.

There are many ways to make some income from your book, if that's your wish. But right now, your priority is to get your words out, to do the work of writing to the very end—to the finish line.

I truly hope your book sells hundreds and thousands and even millions of copies because I want you to make a movement with your words. I know it's possible, as do the thousands of other successful authors across the world. And the more you write, the more it is possible. Never, ever give up on writing. Do what it takes.

Reflection and Action

Review the *why* behind your work.
Set a sales/financial goal accordingly.

31. Remaking the World
On Movement-making

I adore this dialogue between the Cheshire Cat and Alice in *Alice's Adventures in Wonderland* when she reaches a fork in the road and meets the cat.

'Would you tell me, please, which way I ought to go from here?'
'That depends a good deal on where you want to get to,' said the Cat.
'I don't much care where—' said Alice.
'Then it doesn't matter which way you go,' said the Cat.
'—so long as I get somewhere,' Alice added as an explanation.
'Oh, you're sure to do that,' said the Cat, 'if you only walk long enough.'
'In that direction,' the Cat said, waving its right paw round, 'lives a Hatter: and in that direction,' waving the other paw, 'lives a March Hare. Visit either you like: they're both mad.'
'But I don't want to go among mad people,' Alice remarked.
'Oh, you can't help that,' said the Cat: 'we're all mad here. I'm mad. You're mad.'
'How do you know I'm mad?' said Alice.
'You must be,' said the Cat, 'or you wouldn't have come here.'

Welcome to the mad, mad wonderland of the writer's world. You are now here.

We writers truly are a mad lot. Sometimes angry-mad, sometimes crazy-mad but mostly weird-mad. Left-of-centre. Obsessed. Always seeking. Always questioning. Always challenging. Never afraid of feeling all the feelings essential for our work.

Never fear, a little (or even a lot) of madness is the basis of our brilliance. Every time we write, we find ourselves just that little bit madder—and more brilliant. How can we not when every day we're forced to leave home and forge new paths with our words?

But all this is a distraction. A round-about way of sharing that this morning upon waking, I found myself at the crossroads just like Alice ready to go anywhere with my words without much care. I had no idea what road to take, no lead on what story to write, at a standstill.

And then the horrific news that the Taliban had re-taken control of Afghanistan came across the airwaves. There are no words for the tragedy continuing to befall the women, children and families of Afghanistan. I weep for them. I ache for them. I rage for them. I am grief-stricken. I am helpless. I am hopeless. I am all these things.

I do not know why this is happening. I do not know what I can do. I do not know if anything I do here on the other side of the world matters any more. If writing itself doesn't send me mad, then perhaps the insane world we live in will? And then, is there any point to writing at all?

Many times, especially since the pandemic hit, I've wished I was in a more caring profession than writing: nurse, counsellor, paramedic, human-rights lawyer, aid-worker, climate-change scientist or perhaps a doctor. There might be a million and one more helpful jobs I could do to be of service. Why have I not chosen a more useful vocation? Something that would find me working on the ground alongside people and picking up the pieces of our broken planet or preventing it from getting broken in the first place? I've questioned if the world needs more doers and helpers instead of philosophers and writers.

Alas, I'm a mere writer. And, I suppose therefore, a philosopher. For they are inseparable pursuits. My words are the weapon I know how to use best and so, therefore, I'm obliged to use them well.

If writing itself doesn't send me mad, then perhaps the insane world we live in will?

In the end, neither the left nor the right brain won the battle of the subject matter for this chapter. Instinct won instead. My heart sent a message to my gut and it took over. The words came from an unidentifiable, visceral source within. They told me that right now is the very best time to reclaim my purpose, to return to the whole point of this book—to help you, my dear reader, to find your words to help heal your hurt. To urge you to write. To find your voice. To tell your story. To speak up. To march. To fight. To make a movement.

If you haven't yet begun writing, what's the grief you are here to face and heal? What's the message you wish to impart? What are you here to say and who are you here to serve? What do you want to fix with your words? And if you're already well on your way with your words, how do you intend to power them up? What's the change you seek with them? What action will you take to make these words sing with truth?

'The flapping of the wings of a butterfly can be felt on the opposite side of the world,' says a Chinese proverb.

> **Alas, I'm a mere writer. And, I suppose therefore, a philosopher. For they are inseparable pursuits. My words are the weapon I know how to use best and so, therefore, I'm obliged to use them well.**

That's what your writing is for. By sharing your story, you heal yourself and in some small way help heal other women. A neighbour? A co-worker? A friend? And many women you'll never ever get to meet. That's perhaps the greatest intrigue of writing and the very thing that keeps us returning to the page. We may never know who will read our words nor the impact they might have, trusting they'll find just the right human they're meant for.

And hoping against hope that it might be an Afghani woman on the other side of the world.

Our words have the power to remake the world. That's what we're doing with them. We're trying to create a movement of change for a more beautiful world—to add to a movement or start a new one.

I'm most passionate about two movements: the advancement of women's rights and the rights of Mother Earth. It seems to me that they are inextricably entwined, so it was thrilling to learn more about a concept that brings them both together: ecofeminism. Ecofeminism is a philosophical and political theory and movement which combines ecological concerns with feminist activism resulting from male domination.

It's become the cause behind this book. I really didn't know this when I first began to write. That's what writing can do for you. The more you write, the more your cause will reveal itself. What about you? Can you name the cause you want to advance with your words? I urge you to claim it and devote your words to it. Go deep and go hard. Bring your talent and passions together with your cause and watch the movement unfold.

'Don't ask what the world needs. Ask what makes you come alive and go do it. Because what the world needs is people who have come alive,' wrote Howard Thurman, American author and philosopher.

A movement starts by one person finding the courage to reject the dominant systems and beliefs. It starts with that one person questioning the accepted ways and unchecked assumptions and making an alternative idea public—through writing, speaking or marching or whatever form of activism calls you. It starts by that person having a vision of what's possible and then inviting the first followers to join the movement.

A movement doesn't need hundreds of people at first. It just needs a few people committed to the cause. 'Never doubt that a small group of thoughtful, committed citizens can change the world; indeed, it's the only thing that ever has,' wrote American anthropologist and author, Margaret Mead.

Our own Yarra Yabbies movement is a great case study on how to start a movement. It started with one fearless woman, Katie O'Keeffe, questioning the unchecked assumptions, in our case, that our beloved Yarra Birrarung was not safe or suitable for swimming.

> **Starting a movement is risky. But without risk there is no progress. And without movements we cannot build the better world we all crave.**

It starts by that person having a vision of what's possible and then attracting the first followers to trust the leader and join the movement. Soon the risk becomes shared, and so too, does the joy. Then new followers take up the call which eventually makes the movement mainstream. In Katie's case, she actually had no vision to start a movement. She just decided to do something she loves and share it with a few friends. No plans. No expectations. And here we are.

Starting a movement is risky. But without risk there is no progress. And without movements we cannot build the better world we all crave. A movement has to buck the system. It has to go against the flow (pun intended). It must be something people have longed for or offer something that might change their lives in unexpected ways. A movement must test every limiting and unconscious assumption that keeps us restrained and stops us from being brave.

That does not mean the movement is foolhardy or negligent. Our swimming movement is very careful and considered. We swim in pairs or groups. We conduct water-quality tests. We share weather updates. We keep each other informed. We know that we are each responsible for ourselves, but also for each other.

From this movement there have been numerous off-shoot activities that have contributed to the well-being of the river. River clean-up days. A

Welcome to Country ceremony. A Living Yarra Birrarung art exhibition. A contribution to research on how to make the whole of the Yarra Birrarung swimmable. An ABC news story.

Perhaps the most spirited and spiritual aspect of this movement, however, is the transformation we get to witness in each woman as they discover the healing properties of the river. As we emerge from the water, women walking by see the joy on our faces brought on by the hot, tingly, all-over-body sensations. They see their potential new friends transformed and full of vitality, ready for a day of infinite possibilities. They're eager to know more and how it feels and if it's clean and safe.

Sometimes, these women share how much they struggled with lockdown: fatigue, loneliness, depression, the very real impacts of this pandemic. There's a wistfulness, a longing for something—anything—to make daily life more bearable. Often, it's a wish they had the courage to join us. Like most of us, they want to rewire their brain, replenish their soul and get connected to our great, watery earth. And so, one day they find the courage to join us and make the practice a part of their life.

To me, it's ecofeminism in its most embodied and naturalistic form.

Without the pandemic, I suspect I would have remained a public pool swimmer, never experiencing the call to venture into the river in my backyard. Neither would I have made such fabulous new friends. It's the silver lining to the dark cloud of the lockdown. There's no wonder the wild-water swimming movement is sweeping across the ocean shores, swimming holes and waterways of the world.

We don't know how the Yarra Yabbies movement will unfold. That, perhaps, is the point and most enjoyable part of belonging to a movement. You don't need a plan. You don't need rules. You don't need hierarchies. You just need courage, a love of humans and Mother Earth and a deep sense of awe, wonder and adventure. Our Yarra Yabbies swimming group is fast becoming a movement that is remaking our world—one precious human being at a time.

What movement do you wish to make with your words and your actions? Claim it and own it. Find your first followers and make it happen. The world needs you.

Reflection and Action
Name the cause you're advancing and write a
visionary story about the movement you hope to make.

32. Words to Write By
On Your Writer's Manifesto

I'm a big fan of manifestos. Manifestos are statements to live by. They're a written declaration of your intentions for life. A statement of what you desire to be, do, have and give to the world. They articulate what you value and what you stand for. They help you return to what really matters when you find yourself veering off-track—and, of course, when you're feeling stuck in sorrow and grief.

I've had a life manifesto to live by for many years. The famous *Holstee Manifesto* inspired it. I only wish I'd remembered it during my six-month writing-drought. It might have motivated me to get back to my words much earlier than I did.

You can create manifestos for families, couples, partnerships, businesses, communities and schools. I love writing them and have written them as guiding principles for my book *Conscious Marketing* and for the Slow School community.

To create a personal manifesto, use a journaling exercise. Write as many 'I believe . . .' statements as possible.

I believe in doing work that fulfills my purpose.

I believe Mother Earth is in grave harm and that I have a role to play.

I believe my purpose is to write more books that make an impact.

I believe women must be equal to men . . .

Write them until you can write no more. You might end up with more than one hundred statements. You'll find many of the statements cross over or repeat. Then choose the key words from the statements to write your manifesto. It's a fabulous creative exercise and great writing practice.

It was exciting to retrieve my life manifesto and review it. Given my heartbreak, lockdown and this book, it needed an upgrade, so here it is.

My Life Manifesto

Live with purpose. **Do work I love.** BECOME ONE WITH NATURE. Write more books. *Teach with passion.* BE AN ACTIVIST. Advance women's rights. **Fight for the rights of Mother Earth.** BE VULNERABLE. Be brave. *Be bold.* DON'T MIND WHAT OTHERS THINK. Ask excellent questions. **Listen. No, really listen.** SPEAK WISE WORDS. Be kind to others. *Be kind to myself.* INSPIRE OTHERS. Help them find their path. **Guide don't tell.** EXERCISE DAILY. Eat healthily. *Laugh often.* **DO YOGA.** Journal. *Meditate.* **Dance.** READ. Learn. *Swim.* **MAKE SOMEONE'S DAY, EVERY DAY.** Love and nurture my son. **Be a wicked role model for him.** REJOICE IN HIS GROWTH. *Love and serve my community and clients.* Do great things with them. **CELEBRATE SUCCESS.** Create prosperity for all. **Be a loving friend, sister and daughter.** BUILD MY SISTER-TRIBE. Be open to love. **EMBRACE COMMITMENT.** Travel far. **Collect experiences, not things.** ALWAYS REMEMBER HOME. *Rethink. Refuse. Reduce. Re-use. Repair. Recycle.* **CONNECT.** COLLABORATE. **Co-create.** *Remember, love is all there is.*

I hope my manifesto will inspire you to write your own. It takes time, reflection and thought. The best place to write your manifesto is in a creative space or in nature, not at your desk.

And now to another type of manifesto. A writer's manifesto, my next favourite kind. It states your writing philosophy, goals and intentions, your motives, your beliefs, sources of inspiration, what you believe and how to become a greater, braver writer. Here's mine:

My Writer's Life Manifesto

I will **be brave with my words** even if you may not like them.

I will **write to heal myself first** and trust that my words will heal you too.

I will **not write to please you**. I will write to be true to myself first and foremost.

I will **hold you dear to my heart** as I write, however.

I will **write with vulnerability**. I will let you into my world, especially when it's dark.

I will **try not to care too much what you think of me** or my writing.

I will **not compare my writing to others**, for we are incomparable.

I will **strive to show not tell through stories** that inspire you to act.

I will **share my opinions and ideals** with courage and conviction.

I will **try to be kind, compassionate and generous** with my words.

I will **write to advance the cause of women's rights** and the rights of Mother Earth.

I will **unapologetically push you out of your comfort zone**. But we'll be brave together.

I will **do the necessary research** to inform my writing.

I will **learn to write**, and **write to learn**, every single day.

I will **write with the best of intentions** in the best way possible.

I will **accept the gifts** that come through imperfect writing.

I will **seek the company of diverse writers** to challenge my bias and prejudices.

I will **be intrepid with my writing**. I will explore new ideas and expand my repertoire.

I will **write and publish a new book** every two years.

I will **not write to someone else's dictum**. I will decide what I write.

I will **respond to you if you write to me** but I will also protect my time to write.

I will **live a writer's life** until the day I die.

I found pure joy in writing this manifesto. It's given me goosebumps. It's made my heart thump and my stomach churn. That's what a manifesto must do if it is to have any effect. It must cause a gut reaction and a call to action. My writer's manifesto is a work-in-progress. Possibly it's a bit wordy. Maybe that should be in my manifesto. 'I will say more with fewer words.' What do you think? Has it inspired you to write your own?

> **You are the author of your own life. You can write your own future.**

You've no time to spend on it now if you're in flow with your writing project. Feel free to borrow mine to get you through. You can always write your own later.

It occurs to me that an ecofeminist manifesto would be a powerful project for the collective, and one for all women to contribute to and take ownership of. Imagine what might be possible if ecofeminists representing all corners of the world were to co-author a manifesto? 'People support what they create,' says Meg Wheatley, American author and speaker. Perhaps that's a way to advance the movement. I'm sure I'll have an interrupted night's sleep over that one.

You are the author of your own life. You can write your own future. That's what a manifesto is for. You have it in you. If you don't believe you do, 'you can borrow my belief in you, until you have it for yourself,' as my friend, Angela Raspass, says. I do believe in you and the only way to believe in yourself is to do the work of writing. A manifesto might be just the device you need to see you through.

Reflection and Action

Start a section of your journal for your 'I believe … ' statements and make a date with yourself to write your manifestos (either a life manifesto or a writer's life manifesto, or both).

33. The End
On Endings and Beginnings

Can you believe, this first draft manuscript was finished three days before my ninety day lifeline? I just couldn't bring myself to type The End until then though. I'm a little superstitious like that. I never want to jinx myself. I'd planned how it would end and so I must keep my promise.

I did the same for *Unstuck in Provence*. I completed the manuscript before the lifeline and had left the last sentence unwritten with a plan to write it at 11.11am on 01.01.11. The number eleven signifies consciousness, synchronicity and a bright future. I've little knowledge of numerology but it seemed like a portentous way to finish the book.

I'd over-imbibed at a New Year's Eve party the night before which had ended in the wee hours of the morning. Billy had returned home to his father by then so I was on my happy lonesome. I'd stumbled in the door, full of wine and joy—and immense love for my French friends and their country.

After a few hours' sleep, I arose and wrote the final words still tipsy and taking comfort in the knowing I could edit sober later. I typed The End at 11.11am before heading out the door to a celebration with a hair-of-the-dog and a long lunch with friends. It was the final day of my sabbatical and I was to depart Aix the following morning.

Two major conclusions occurred in unison: the end of my book and the end of my French adventure. So, as you can imagine, my emotions were running hot and high. One minute I was jubilant, the next miserable.

Endings occur because something new must begin. There can be no beginnings without endings and no endings without beginnings. Less than profound, I admit, however I think at times, we humans can feel like we're stuck in some endless, monotonous existence that drags on and on until we die. We lack the sense of the vitality that can come from living life as a series of purpose-driven projects, each with a start and a finish.

As you near the end of your work, it's time to go back to the beginning, to read the first few chapters and remind yourself of what first brought you to the keyboard. Just the first few though. Go no further. Its sole purpose is so you can appreciate just how far you've progressed in your writing practice—and just how much you've healed.

Reading my own first chapters was illuminating. They reminded me that I began this book as a means to recover from my broken heart and return from my six-month writing exile. I had to do something radical to step out of my wordless and loveless life—and depression.

It's always personal. Always. Writers write to heal. It's the ultimate purpose of our art, no matter our writing inclinations.

So, has writing this book done the trick for me? The answer is YES—more than I could have ever hoped or planned for. I can't begin to describe the many ways it's helped. What about you? Has writing done the trick for you too?

I deliberately avoided revealing all the excruciating details of the relationship in this book. Nor did I choose to air too much of my anguish through the narrative, despite it often being palpable and overwhelming. I refused to let it overpower my words. Instead, I used the private ache to fuel my words. Without some pain, I've come to learn, there is no great work.

I still have love for this man, despite no contact since that fateful day in the park. However, my heart hurts no more. And the longing I had for him has vanished. I've fully accepted that we are done.

> **Endings occur because something new must begin. There can be no beginnings without endings and no endings without beginnings.**

I will always have love for him. That is just how it will be. Just because he is out of my life, does not mean I love him less. And I'm happy that my heart was cracked open to love and sad for him that he never got to experience fully loving me. There are always winners and losers in the game of love and if I had to pick a winner today, I would pick me.

Just as I will soon type The End on this book, I can now, with dignity and certainty, type The End on him—and us.

You must set a date and a plan for what will happen after you type The End on your work. Determine how you'll pay homage to your commitment and accomplishment. Crossing the finish line of your writing project is a euphoric feeling. It's an achievement to covet and celebrate. Please do not let this momentous occasion slip by without acknowledgement. Make it a grand or private gesture to yourself. Be sure to honour and savour the moment.

I was going to pay homage to ending this manuscript with a three-day camping trip with friends, as I've already shared. Alas lockdown killed our plans. No matter, I plan to celebrate with a bottle of champagne and a home-cooked meal with my son tonight.

> **For it's in this void where your greatest growth occurs as your completed work takes root in your whole being. You can now live your words instead of just writing them.**

While The End is a time to celebrate, it also marks the beginning of a period of mourning. With a few clicks of the keyboard, you're suddenly losing your most beloved and constant companion, perhaps the only friend that's soothed your sorrow and saved your sanity for months. A project that has kept you focused and fulfilled in equal measures.

At The End you must let go and accept that you will never recapture the wild, precious experience you've just had. You will never feel the restorative flow of such writing in quite the same way. As you celebrate your victory, you mourn your loss.

You will feel like Alice emerging from the White Rabbit's burrow back into the real world. You will find yourself stepping into an uncomfortable void. The vacuum may leave you wistfully looking back at the warren wondering if you might scuttle back down. Or it might leave you hopping right on to the next stage and polishing your work into something useful for others.

After the loss, however, comes liberation. You have had a transformational adventure. Word by word, day by day and story by story, you have become a new woman. Something is different about you. Something more palpable and powerful that was always within but had remained hidden, has revealed itself.

I recommend staying in the void for exactly one month. Do not go backwards. Do not go forwards. Do not re-open your work. Take no action with your words. Reconnect with the world beyond your writing burrow. Forget your words for a while.

For it's in this void where your greatest growth occurs as your completed work takes root in your whole being. You can now live your words instead of just writing them.

In this void, you will notice new possibilities emerging. You'll be forced to shed what's been holding you back and step towards something new. You'll find yourself no longer stuck in your old stories and ready to create a new story—not just for you, but for all women and for Mother Earth.

You will have choices to make and action to take. Small evolutionary acts. Or big bold revolutionary ones. Often both. There will be endings. And there will be beginnings. And all of it will require courage.

Because, just as brave women write, brave women act.

May I have the courage today
To live the life that I would love
To postpone my dream no longer
But do at last what I came here for
And waste my heart on fear no more.

John O'Donohue, Irish poet and philosopher
The End

Reflection and Action
Paint a vision of how you'll celebrate when you type
The End.

Epilogue
Truth Be Known

One month after typing The End on this manuscript, a serendipitous opportunity to write the second draft presented itself.

My friend, Deb Rayner, and I began renting a magical cabin in the charming Victorian town of Warburton from a friend, Corinne Willowson. Warburton is just an hour's drive from Melbourne upstream on the Yarra Birrarung river. It was on a short-term three-month basis with us sharing the week between us. I would have three days of uninterrupted time to devote myself to writing with nature right outside my door—and the nearby river to swim in every day.

On the first day, as I was waiting for my stove-top coffee to brew, I set up a desk in front of the expansive window overlooking pale-pink apple blossoms and the tumbling waters of La La Creek. Fire alight, Nils Frahm playlist on, candle aglow, I needed nothing else to complete my cosy writer's den.

With short-black in hand, I sat with great expectation at my desk. After twenty minutes of reading, despair descended. I stood, plodded outside and slumped by the creek, soaking my bare feet in its frigid flow. My heart felt like one of the creek's ponderous stones. I had not an ounce of enthusiasm for my words.

Even some hours later after a forest-walk, a river-swim and a slumberous afternoon, I was still struggling to motivate myself. A kind of melancholic apathy had set in.

You might find this too when you return to your work. Try not to let it get the better of you. And if it does, like it did with me for that whole three months in Warburton, do something worthy to fill the time and trust you'll get back to it when the moment is right.

So, despite me urging you to jump right back into your writing project after exactly one month, I couldn't do it myself.

While I couldn't rekindle my love for the manuscript during my time in Warburton, I did develop a deeper and more profound love and connection to the natural world—and the river. A love I likely would never have discovered if I'd turned over every waking hour to this book.

> **It felt like invisible threads were being woven between the river, their stories and mine.**

It was not long after the end of the last lockdown and so Mother Nature was calling me to forget my writing plans and join with her instead. I heeded her call rather than trying to plough on regardless. I know now that I just wasn't meant to be deskbound for those months. I was meant to be devoting myself to Gaia and practising Dadirri (deep listening).

If I wasn't going to write, at least I could read. And I did, a lot. Two books written by sister-Victorians had a profound impact on me: *Rewilding the Urban Soul* by Claire Dunn and the *Comfort of Water* by Maya Ward. The first explores how we can find deep nature connections amid the concrete and busyness of city-living. The second follows the author's pilgrimage from the sea to the source of the Yarra Birrarung.

It felt like invisible threads were being woven between the river, their stories and mine.

As it turned out, my nature and river immersions and Claire's and Maya's stories were the fuel needed for this book to become better, bolder and braver through the second and third drafts in the ensuing twelve months.

I'm happy now that I didn't rush it and thrust it into the world prematurely. It needed time and thought to ripen into a book I would be proud of, one that would be more helpful to my readers. I also needed time and distance from the end of love, the very thing that had brought me to the page in the first place.

So beware. This might happen to you after you type The End and sit in the void.

If you pay attention and heed what's calling you, you might just experience the most profound transformation. All sorts of events might occur. A stream of unforeseen incidents, people and opportunities may arise, events that you could not have conceived of as you first began to write, events that you may have no choice but to say YES to. You'll begin to live your brave words in real-life.

And then this will give you inspiration for your next big writing project. Guaranteed.

For me, there's something in the ninety-day theory. Ninety days to write the first draft. Ninety days in nature, no writing. Ninety days to write the second draft. Ninety days to let it percolate. Then ninety days to publish and launch. See what you might make of it for your own writing projects.

And now back to the source, where it all began and must finish. Grief. Our hearts are made to be broken. We can't avoid it. And nor would we want to. Over and over they break until our dying day. There is a way to transform our grief into gold.

Writing is the way.

Recommended Reading

Australian Society of Authors
Block, Peter, *Community: The structure of belonging.*
Brown, Brené, *Daring Greatly*
Cameron, Julia, *The Artist's Way*
Campbell, Joseph, *The Hero with a Thousand Faces. (Novato: New World Library, 2008)*
Carroll, Lewis, *Alice's Adventures in Wonderland*
Clarke, Roy Peter, *How to Write Short: Word Craft for Fast Times*
Dunn, Claire, *Rewilding the Urban Soul*
Frankl, Viktor, *Man's Search for Meaning*
Gibran, Kahlil, *The Prophet*
Gilbert, Elizabeth, *Big Magic*
Gilbert, Elizabeth, *Eat Pray Love*
Goldberg, Natalie, *Writing Down the Bones*
Gottlieb, Lori, *Maybe you Should Talk to Someone*
Hari, Johann, *Lost Connections: Uncovering the Real Causes of Depression and the Surprising Solutions*
Jeffers, Susan, *Feel the Fear and Do it Anyway*
Jenkinson, Stephen, *Come of Age*
King, Stephen, *On Writing*
Lamott, Anne, *Bird by Bird*
Louv, Richard, *Last Child in the Woods: Saving Our children from Nature-Deficit Disorder*
Macy, Joanna and Johnstone, Chris, *Active Hope: How to face the mess we're in without going crazy.*
Murdock, Maureen, *The Heroine's Journey*
Smith, Patti, *Just Kids*
Steinem, Gloria, *Life on the Road*
The Holstee Manifesto

Ueland, Brenda, *If you want to write: A book about art, independence and spirit*
Walters, Kath, *Overnight Authority*
Ward, Maya, *The Comfort of Water*
Ware, Bronnie, *The Top Five Regrets of the Dying*
Watson, Don, *Watson's Dictionary of Weasel Words*
Weller, Francis, *The Wild Edge of Sorrow*
Woolf, Virginia, *A Room of One's Own*
World Economic Forum, The Global Gender Gap Research

Other books by Carolyn Tate

The Purpose Project

A handbook for bringing meaning to life.

Bring your *why* to work. Start where you are.

A higher purpose than profit is now an imperative for a thriving workplace. Purpose answers the fundamental questions. 'Why are we here? What is most meaningful to us? How is the world better because we exist? What is the legacy we are leaving?'

The Purpose Project is a practical handbook, filled with models, real-life stories and practices for business leaders, employees, entrepreneurs and students who are committed to bringing meaning to life at work. The book shows you how to integrate your personal work purpose with the higher purpose of your organisation, starting right where you are, right now.

Personal purpose: Work with the Japanese Ikigai model and fifty self reflection questions to find your why and bring it to work (BYO Purpose).

Organisational purpose: Learn how to become a Purpose Activist to co-create and co-activate your company purpose so that everyone takes responsibility for it.

The 12 practices of purpose: Discover how to become a practitioner of purpose through twelve essential practices such as finding courage, curiosity, creativity and re-learning.

The Purpose Project: Commit to your own personal and organisational purpose projects to experiment with your why and step boldly onto the path to purpose.

Conscious Marketing

How to create an awesome business with a new approach to marketing.

Conscious Marketing teaches you how to bring a higher purpose to marketing your business that can benefit customers, employees, investors, suppliers and the community. Through innovative principles and in-depth case studies, this book shows you how to turn your business into a movement that people want to join.

With decades of experience in business and marketing, author, Carolyn Tate, presents a model that will show you how to:

- Define your company's purpose as the central force for all your marketing activities

- Build a community that is truly inspired to help you grow your business

- Create compelling products and services that your customers love to buy

- Make your promotional activities less costly and more effective.

Drawing on the values from the 'slow' and 'conscious' business movements, *Conscious Marketing* will help you build a business that can grow your bottom line while serving the community.

Unstuck in Provence

The courage to start over.

At the age of forty-six, after years of single motherhood and the unbearable feeling that life is going nowhere, author, Carolyn Tate, decides to get radically unstuck.

After selling her home, giving away most of her belongings, putting her flagging business on hold and ending a destructive love affair, she takes her twelve-year-old son, Billy, to live in Aix-en-Provence, France.

Carolyn's raw and real daily diary entries reveal how she goes about healing herself and recovering her spirituality, creativity and self-love. The pages also explore her occasionally tense but tender relationship with Billy, a boy on the cusp of becoming a teenager.

If you've ever needed the inspiration or courage to get unstuck—to shake off whatever it is in your life that prevents you from becoming the woman you were destined to be—*Unstuck in Provence* is for you.

www.ingramcontent.com/pod-product-compliance
Lightning Source LLC
Chambersburg PA
CBHW072010030526
44107CB00092B/2580